WESTVILLE

Tales from a Connecticut Hamlet

COLIN M. CAPLAN

Published by The History Press
Charleston, SC 29403
www.historypress.net

Copyright © 2009 by Colin M. Caplan
All rights reserved

Cover image: Old Mill at Hotchkisstown, circa 1825. *Painted by John Rubens Smith. Courtesy of the Library of Congress.*

First published 2009

ISBN 9781540229281

Library of Congress Cataloging-in-Publication Data
Caplan, Colin M.
Westville : tales from a Connecticut hamlet / [compiled by] Colin M. Caplan.
p. cm.
ISBN 9781540229281
1. Westville (New Haven, Conn.)--History--19th century. 2. New Haven (Conn.)--History--19th century. 3. Westville (616.8, Conn.)--History--20th century. 4. New Haven (Conn.)--History--20th century. 5. Westville (New Haven, Conn.)--Social life and customs. 6. New Haven (Conn.)--Social life and customs. 7. Westville (New Haven, Conn.)--Biography. 8. New Haven (Conn.)--History--Biography. 9. American newspapers--Connecticut--New Haven. I. Title.
F104.N657C374 2008
974.6'8--dc22
2008049164

Notice: The information in this book is true and complete to the best of our knowledge. It is offered without guarantee on the part of the author or The History Press. The author and The History Press disclaim all liability in connection with the use of this book.
All rights reserved. No part of this book may be reproduced or transmitted in any form whatsoever without prior written permission from the publisher except in the case of brief quotations embodied in critical articles and reviews.

CONTENTS

Acknowledgements	5
Introduction	7
Settlement and Judge's Cave	9
The British Attack	18
The Pirate of Hotchkisstown	23
Industry, Inventions, Fires and Floods	38
Life in Westville	53
Murder and Mayhem	86
The Grand Estates	105
Growth of a Suburb	118

ACKNOWLEDGEMENTS

I would like to thank the following for their contributions to this book: Gil Gershman for diligently and swiftly editing and transcribing most of the old texts; the New Haven Free Public Library for its assistance with researching the old articles; the New Haven Museum & Historical Society for its help with research and supplying some old photographs; the *New Haven Register* for its generosity in granting the reproduction of many of its articles and Joseph Taylor for supplying photographs and for his persistent energy in educating others in our local history; and Grace and Irving, Harriet and Arthur, Francine and Bob, Amy and Nico and Crissy for everything else.

INTRODUCTION

Westville, unlike other sections of New Haven, remained a distinct town until it was absorbed into the city of New Haven in 1921. With its village charm, rich history, intense manufacturing and colorful characters, the village blossomed into a thriving, wealthy suburb. To fully understand the history of this bustling hamlet we must delve deep into its old stories. These stories tell of pirates, invasions, floods, fires, murders and general town gossip. We can understand modern-day Westville by experiencing a connection to the people who once lived there. The original articles used in this book paint a picture of day-to-day life in Westville.

This book incorporates multiple texts from the nineteenth and early twentieth centuries. They include articles from six different newspapers, magazines, pamphlets, ledgers and books. The accounts were, in many cases, written as they happened. They pinpoint obscure but important events in local history and reveal the cyclical occurrence of events in nature. Other articles and extracts are accounts of what was already considered historical discourse at the time they were written.

There are so many reasons why using these primary sources to tell the history of Westville adds to its historical accountability. Instead of relying solely on the editing and commentary of this modern author, we are exposed to the language, morality, sway and eloquence of different, often unidentified authors, performing their jobs by reporting what they saw and heard. This permits for a more valid and profound historical essay than the traditional history where too much is left to authors' discretion; facts get left out or obscured based on their intentional or ignorant judgment. If the reader, after fully participating in this book to the end, finds that there are some major gaps, expect a sequel based on those unpublished stories.

Similar to a traditional history, the chapters in this book are ordered chronologically and by major themes in Westville's history. In between the articles are the author's commentary and explanations. These notes are

Westville was a little hamlet with rivers and brooks running through grassy fields in the shadow of a soaring cliff. Its first residents in the mid-seventeenth century included Richard Sperry and Sheriff Joshua Hotchkiss, who lived in what was the wilderness frontier of western New Haven. By the mid-eighteenth century, the town boasted numerous mills and was a self-sustaining community. *Woodcut by Richardson-Cox. Courtesy of Colin M. Caplan.*

provided to elucidate the old firsthand accounts. Minimal editorial work was done to change the old grammar and spelling in these texts, but their cadence and language are surprisingly readable and refreshing.

SETTLEMENT AND JUDGE'S CAVE

The beginnings of Westville are very closely related to what continues to attract people there these days. The perching red cliffs of West Rock and the numerous springs and rivers have provided wonderment, power and material. Prior to recorded history, this was the land of the Wepawaug, Paugussett and Quinnipiac people. But the English Puritans found a home for their runaway colony nearby at New Haven in 1638 and the land was divided up between the settlers' families.

The land that is now Westville was first divided up in 1640–41 and was sold to the larger and more prominent families of New Haven. The land was originally called Westfield due to its location and its intended use as fields for grazing and growing. The first resident of Westfield was Richard Sperry, a farmer whose house was located along what is now the Litchfield Turnpike in the Amity section.

Another early resident was Sheriff Joshua Hotchkiss, who, in 1677, moved to what is now the area of Whalley Avenue and Blake Street in "downtown" Westville. Here began generations of Hotchkisses who built their houses, stores and mills in this vicinity. Due to their predominance, the little village was called Hotchkisstown. Other early residents of the area include Ralph Lines, Captain John Munson, John Cooper and Abraham Dickerman.

AMERICA'S SPERRYS SPRANG FROM OLD WESTVILLE HOME

New Haven Journal-Courier, June 1934
By Everett Whitlock

No more charming bit of old New England has come down to us than this old painting. We find more here than a still landscape—it has life and personality. The boy plodding in knee-deep snow, hands in his pockets, the bundled up gentleman in his business sleigh and the farmer driving his wood sledge supply an actual winter street scene of long ago. The artist has caught the gray coldness of the morning so that we almost wish we might step into the old saltbox house, bespeaking of hominess, warmth and cheer. The canvas, as may be said of all Durrie's work, presents the peace and quiet of living that we today associate, rightly or wrongly, with life of those times. He makes it seem not sentimental but actual. The artist could well have repaired the broken rail in the fence, but his scene would then have been an unreal.

However, the interest of the picture rests not alone in artistic merit, for the old house, until it was destroyed by fire some years ago, was the old Sperry homestead, from which sprang the thirty-six thousand Sperrys in America today. It was located in Hotchkisstown, now Westville, under the bluffs of West Rock. Here came to pass events that are not only history of New Haven, but of our country.

The land on which the old house stood is part of the original farm bought by the Sperry ancestor, Richard Sperry, from Stephen Goodyear in 1640. The old deed, ambiguous as most of them were, gave all the land between the two mountain ranges, extending to the south to the river that runs through Westville and "as far north as the good land goeth." It is this Richard who is the farmer mentioned in the records as feeding the regicides, Whalley and Goffe, while they were hiding in Judge's Cave in 1660, about whom the Reverend John Davenport had preached from the text, "Hide the outcast, betray not him that wandereth."

It was in this old house that there lived another Richard Sperry, colonel in the Revolutionary army, whose memory is kept alive by legends that have come down to us. Richard, it seems, was at home when the British raided New Haven. They were entering Westville on their way to New Haven when the colonel saw them. He, with his flintlock, was hiding behind a fencepost. He fired once, dropped a Britisher, ran into the house before they knew what happened, kissed his wife and beat it for New Haven, where he joined the Patriots.

Here, too, at a later date lived Merritt N. Sperry and Susan L., his wife. Merritt was a blacksmith by trade who used to keep his accounts on the wall in chalk. It is related that his wife, wanting to surprise him when he was away, decided to clean the shop and carefully scrubbed all the walls.

"Susan," he shouted when he returned, "you have ruined me."

"It's all right," he said about an hour later. "I have a lot of better names on those doors than you washed off."

Going back to 1660, when Richard Sperry fed the regicides, West Rock and its surroundings were untamed wilderness full of giant old trees, deer, fox, wolves, bears and mountain lions. The cave was more of a shelter created by the cavities inside of a giant cracked boulder. The boulder was originally set there by glaciers and cracked into smaller pieces by frost heaving.

THE REGICIDES

Outline History of New Haven, 1884
By Henry Howe

After the restoration of the monarchy in England, three of the judges—Goffe, Whalley and Dixwell—who had condemned Charles I fled for their lives to this country. Goffe and Whalley arrived in Boston in 1660 and, not feeling safe there, next year came to New Haven and were kindly entertained by Mr. Davenport and others, the people universally sympathizing with them. While here two messengers of the Crown were sent to arrest them and they secreted themselves in various places. The most prominent of these was "Judge's Cave," on the summit of West Rock, which is not a cave, but a cluster of five boulders—the tallest about sixteen feet high—which, leaning together, form a small cavity underneath. While there they were daily sent food by Richard Sperry, who lived about a mile away in front of the mountain. Another hiding place was at the "Lodge" or "Hatchet Harbor," a spot shown today in Woodbridge, about seven miles from the city. High on the tallest of the boulders at Judge's Cave, from time immemorial, has been seen this line, though now nearly, if not quite, obliterated:

Disobedience to Tyrants is Obedience to God!

True Story of the Regicides

Saturday Chronicle, April 6, 1918
By P. Henry Woodward
"Connecticut's Active Interest in Beheading King Charles I—Exiled Son Vows Vengeance on Judges Who Signed Death Warrant"

On January 30, 1641, King Charles I was beheaded, fifty-nine of the judges who sat at the trial having signed the death warrant. In the spring of 1660, his son, Charles II, was called from exile to the throne. With the death of Cromwell, its great leader, the power of the revolutionary party passed away. Weary of austerities and strife, a fickle generation joyously threw the powers torn from the father into the hands of the son.

Of the judges, three were brought to the scaffold by the baseness of a Puritan renegade from Massachusetts. Three, finding an asylum in New England, escaped the vengeance of the Crown.

Edward Whalley, first cousin of Oliver Cromwell and John Hampden, rose through all grades to the rank of lieutenant general by valor on many battlefields. He had custody of the king during his captivity at Hampton Court, and on his escape Charles left a farewell letter acknowledging his courtesy. He was a member of the second and third Parliaments of Cromwell and by him was called up to "the other house."

William Goffe, son-in-law of Whalley, among other services, commanded Cromwell's regiment at the battle of Dunbar, greatly pleased the protector by vigor in the second purging of Parliament, succeeded to the command of Lambert as major general of foot, served in two Parliaments, like Whalley was called up to Cromwell's House of Lords and was one of the main supporters of Richard Cromwell during his brief term.

Late in November, news reached Boston that Whalley and Goffe were not embraced in the pardon. Alarm seized the leaders of the colony. Fear overmastered inclination. On February 22, 1661, Governor Endicott called together the court of assistants to consult about securing them, but the court declined to act. Four days later the judges vanished. On March 8, when it was known that the fugitives had passed beyond the jurisdiction of the province, the authorities issued a warrant for their arrest. This was sent to Springfield and other outlying towns, rather to manufacture evidence for use in London than to intercept the flight.

On March 7 the judges arrived at New Haven, the only town in the colonies that could offer hope of safety at this critical juncture. The wife of Reverend William Hook, the associate of John Davenport in the ministry of the local church from 1644 to 1656, was sister to Whalley and hence related to several of the leading spirits in the Cromwellian party. Another resident, William Jones, deputy governor of Connecticut from 1691 to 1697, son of Colonel William Jones, the regicide who had already died on the scaffold, cherished an ardent love for the lost cause. Reverend John Davenport, driven from England by religious persecution, father of the settlement and a leader of such caliber that the political and ideological evolution of the New Haven colony during the entire period of its independence was a reflex of his personal force, at the peril of estate, liberty and even life gave refuge to the judges in his house and inspired his associates with the resolve to shelter them at all hazards. About the time of their arrival he preached from the text Isaiah 91:3-4: "Take counsel, execute judgment, make thy shadow as the night in the midst of the noonday; hide the outcasts; betray not him that wandereth. Let mine outcasts dwell with thee. Moab, be thou a cover to them from the face of the spoiler."

Just two months after the judges reached New Haven, or on May 7, Thomas Kellond and Thomas Kirke, young royalists lately from England and armed with a mandate from the king and a warrant from Governor Endicott, left Boston in pursuit. At Hartford they were politely received by Governor Winthrop and told that the judges made no stay there, but went directly on to New Haven. Having arranged plans with the Dutch governor for the apprehension of the judges, should opportunity offer, they returned by sea to Boston. Their written report to Governor Endicott bears the date of May 29, 1661.

A meeting of the commissioners of the United Colonies held in Hartford on September 5 issued a declaration setting forth that diligent search had been made for Whalley and Goffe in the several colonies, warning all persons not to harbor them and to give to the nearest governor or magistrate any information they either have or may obtain, on peril of being accounted public enemies.

After the friends most deeply interested advised against a voluntary surrender, the judges returned to the cave, not venturing far away until August 10, when they removed to Milford.

Late in July 1664, the royal commission, headed by Colonel Richard Nichols, arrived in Boston. Fearing a renewal of the search, and known in Milford, the judges returned to the cave on West Rock. After eight or ten days, a party of Indians discovered their bed and spread the news. Trusty friends again intervened. In October, traveling only by night, the judges removed to Hadley, Massachusetts.

In February 1665, the regicides at Hadley had a visit from another signer of the death warrant, Colonel John Dixwell. About 1671, he appeared in

Two soldiers who fought in the Union army during the Civil War rest atop the jumble of erratic boulders known as Judge's Cave. The view is from a stereographic view from around 1868. For three weeks in 1661, three exiled judges who sentenced to death King Charles I of England found refuge under these rocks. *Photographed by Henry S. Peck. Courtesy of Colin M. Caplan.*

New Haven under the name of James Davids. Where he lived during the years of exile that preceded and followed the call at Hadley no one knows. Governor Jones recognized the stranger as a person he had seen in youth among the magnates of London. To him, the secret was sacred. It does not appear that his presence in New Haven was ever suspected by agents of the Crown. Like Goffe, he corresponded with English friends through the hands of Reverend Increase Mather. His monument bears the inscription:

J. D. Esq.
Deceased March ye 18th
In ye 82d year of his age, 1688.

Mary Dixwell, the only descendant of John then surviving, in 1774 married Samuel Hunt, master of the famous Latin grammar school of Boston. Their son, John, by legislative act, took the name of Dixwell.

At the demolition of the Russell house in Hadley in 1795, the bones of a large man, presumably Whalley, were uncovered in the cellar. The ashes of Goffe rest in an unknown grave, probably in Hartford.

CUT NINETY YEARS AGO

New Haven Register, September 30, 1893
To the Editor of the *Register*, by Henry T. Blake
"The Inscription on Judge's Cave: The 'Modern Hand' the Late Dr. Bacon Spoke of Was That of Reverend Isaac Jones—Distinguished Man Who Have Visited West Rock—The Inscription Touched Up"

Probably very few of the many visitors to Judge's Cave in West Rock Park have been aware up to the present time that there has existed upon in for nearly a century a quaint inscription as follows:

> OPOSITION TO
> TYRANTS IS
> OBEDIENCE TO
> GOD

The single P in "opposition" is not a misspelling; it has a line over it denoting the contraction of a double letter, which was common one hundred years ago and is to be seen occasionally on ancient tombstones.

This inscription, nearly obliterated by time and other markings, has recently been plainly brought out by painting the incision, and forms an interesting feature in this historic pile. Its origin and date have long been disputed, and therefore definite information as to both will be acceptable to the public.

I have in my possession a slip cut from the *Litchfield Enquirer* of March 25, 1846, which not only settles the questions above referred to, but gives additional facts connected with the history of the cave not generally known. It is a communication from Reverend Isaac Jones, a descendant of Governor

Jones, one of the early governors of New Haven, and through him also of Governor Eaton, the first governor, of whom Governor Jones was the son-in-law. The first half of the paper contains a description of the cave and an account of the judges, and the communication continues as follows:

> In the early part of the summer of 1794 this Cave of the Judges was visited by the writer of the above in company with Mr. Bomar, a French gentleman of distinction, and Charles Maurice Perigord Talleyrand, bishop of Antun in France. In ascending the steep acclivity of the mountain the latter complained of lameness and fatigue, and accompanied the writer of this, aged 19, arm in arm till he reached the summit. Upon their entrance Talleyrand made a very animated and impassioned address in French in relation to those British exiles, their amor patria, and their love of freedom.
>
> The Rev. Dr. Bacon, in his memoir of the Center Brick church, having described the protection of the judges by the men of New Haven and in particular by Davenport and Jones, in relation to their place of seclusion correctly and vividly observes:
>
> "The rude munition of rocks that sheltered the fugitives when they were chased into dens and caves of the earth is a monument more eloquent than arch or obelisk. Till the mountains shall melt, let it bear the inscription:
>
> 'OPPOSITION TO TYRANTS IS OBEDIENCE TO GOD'
>
> He subjoins in a note below: "The inscription cited above was placed upon the Judge's Cave by modern hand."
>
> The modern hand here mentioned, and by whom it was done, was the writer of this sketch. On his return from Washington, Wilkes county, Ga., to New Haven, May 22d, 1803, he was accompanied by Mr. James A. Meriwether, son of the Hon. David Meriwether, then a member of congress, and in whose mansion he had resided. Soon after he had returned in company with this talented and promising young gentleman, who had been his pupil at Washington academy, he visited the cave June, 1803, and glowing with the same spirit that animated his venerated ancestor, cut in the rock the above-mentioned inscription. After some months' absence Mr. Meriwether returned to Georgia. He graduated at Athens university. He has been elected member of congress from his native state and has but very recently retired from that distinguished body. Hon. James A. Meriwether is

well known to the American public for the distinguished part he took in advocating the claims of the Hon. Henry Clay to the presidency of the United States.
—Isaac Jones, rector of Trinity Church, Milton, Litchfield, Connecticut, March 25, 1846

The interest that Talleyrand took in the cave and the regicides will be easily understood when it is remembered that he had only the year before (1793) witnessed the execution of Louis XCI, at Paris, and was himself at that time a political exile. President Stiles's *History of the Judges* also had been then published by only a few months, so that the cave was at that time a special local celebrity. I have not been able to learn anything of his companion, "Mr. Bomar," though referred to in the above as "a French gentleman of distinction."

There is a tradition that Talleyrand narrowly escaped drowning while crossing the Housatonic River by the ancient ferry near the present Milford and Stratford bridge, but I know nothing of its authenticity.

THE BRITISH ATTACK

Invasion of New Haven

Outline History of New Haven, 1884
By Henry Howe

The great military event in the history of New Haven was its invasion, Monday, July 5, 1779, by the British then in possession of New York. The troops were under the command of Major General Tryon and numbered about 2,600 men. The narrative annexed is abridged from the diary of President Stiles of Yale College.

About one o'clock on the morning of July 5, the fleet of about forty sail, under Sir George Collier, anchored off West Haven. Alarm guns were fired and Lieutenant Colonel Sabin ordered to beat to arms. With a telescope on the top of the tower of the college steeple, we plainly saw the boats putting off from the shipping for shore a little after sunrise. All then knew our fate. Perhaps one-third of the adult male inhabitants flew to arms and went out to meet them. A quarter moved out of town, doing nothing; the rest remained unmoved, partly Tories, partly timid Whigs. Sundry of the Tories armed and went forth to fight the foe. About ninety or one hundred men finally stayed in town.

At five o'clock in the morning General Garth's division landed at West Haven and marched to the meetinghouse, one mile, and formed upon the Green, where they halted two hours. About nine or ten, General Tryon landed his division at Five-Mile Point. Both divisions were engaged in their respective operations: Tryon approaching the town on the east side of the harbor and Garth on the west. Colonel Sabin with two pieces of artillery went to West Bridge. Captain James Hillhouse, with twenty or thirty brave young men, together with many others, crossed West Bridge, went over Milford Hill and thence within a quarter of a mile of the Green where

Southeastern view of West Rock and Westville. This 1836 view was sketched from present-day Whalley and West Park Avenues, east of Westville. This road became widely used after it was incorporated as part of the Litchfield Turnpike in 1797, when the road was first bridged over the West River. The British cavalry forded the river and followed this road into New Haven during their siege on July 5, 1779. *Woodcut by John W. Barber. Courtesy of Colin M. Caplan.*

the enemy were paraded. Upon their beginning the march, Captain James Hillhouse fired upon the advance guard so as to drive them in to the main body. But coming in force, the enemy perceived others besides Hillhouse's party had by this time passed the bridge and reached the hill, perhaps to the number of 150 men. These kept up a galling fire, especially on their outguards or skirmishers, extending perhaps to about forty rods each side of the column; and yet the column marched vigorously, but in a huddled confusion—about thirty companies, in three divisions.

On Milford Hill their adjutant, Colonel Campbell, was slain. Sundry more were wounded. Reverend Dr. Napthali Daggett (ex-president of Yale College) was captured. Our artillery at the bridge (Allingtown), was well served by Captain Phineas Bradley, and prevented the enemy passing the causeway and so into town that way. So they turned off and continued their route round to Derby Bridge (now Westville Bridge). As they came along our people divided: some crossed the bridge; others kept to the enemy's left, and under command of Colonel Aaron Burr (afterward vice-president of the United States), harassed the enemy's march. When it was seen that they were aiming for the bridge (Westville), Captains Hillhouse and Bradley, with the artillery, crossed the fields to meet them. The main body crossed the bridge, the rest fording the river. Then, on the enemy rising the hill on this side and taking the road to town, we gave them a hearty fire and took a number of prisoners; also, on the other side we took a number.

The northern militia and those from Derby by this time pressed in and passed on all sides, and some behaved with amazing intrepidity. One captain drew up and threw his whole company (the Derby company, probably) directly before the enemy's column, and gave and received their fire. We fought upon a retreat into the town. Just at the northwest Ditch Corner entrance to town the battle became very severe and bloody for a short time, when a number were killed on both sides. [This was just beyond Broadway, where the fire alarm tower now stands, on Goffe Street.] The enemy, however, passed on in force and entered town a little past noon. From that time the town was given up to ravage and plunder, from which only a few houses were protected.

When the British left the city to embark, Tuesday morning about sunrise, some of the officers were seen driving their drunken, red-coated soldiers across the Green, striking them with the flats of their swords. As we now look upon that peaceful, delight-giving spot, we cannot realize that it was ever the scene of such a performance. A very handsome picture of that time is given by one of our home-writers, Reverend Chauncey Goodrich, grandson of Hon. Elizur Goodrich, whom we have just quoted. It gives the appearance of the British marching through what we now call Westville, as seen from the top of West Rock. He writes:

> Some persons who had fled from New Haven to the houses near West Rock, ascended the rock, and from its summit viewed the march of the British as they advanced and entered the west end of the village. One of the number in after years described the sight as very striking, and even beautiful. The long column of men moving with the regular step of disciplined troops; the mingling colors of the uniforms worn—the bright red of the English Foot Guards blending with the graver hues of the dress worn by the German Mercenaries; the waving line of glistening bayonets; the hurried riding forth and back of mounted officers, and the frequent flashes of musketry, no doubt combined to make up a scene which might still attract admiration, were not the occasion so fraught with terror to the spectators.

The British intended to destroy at least one of the two powder houses. General Garth sent a small detachment of troops down Valley Street to destroy the mill, but townspeople of

The British Attack

During the British raid on Westville, British and Hessian troops marched down this road, Valley Street, in order to take control of one of the militia's powder mills located behind the houses. The invaders were pushed back and many were taken captive. This circa 1907 photograph shows the Captain Jonathan Mix house, built circa 1775, on the left-hand side and the Elijah Thompson House, circa 1787, on the right. *Photographed by T.S. Bronson. Courtesy of the New Haven Museum & Historical Society.*

This circa 1880 photograph is looking south down Forest Road from the present corner of Willard Street. The old house at the head of the road's curve was built for Isaac Dickerman in 1779, soon after the British troops marched down the road during their raid of Westville and New Haven on July 5, 1779. *Courtesy of Joseph Taylor.*

all ages and the militia from Derby made a valiant show of force. The British attempted twice to take the powder mill and then returned to an adjacent paper mill operated by Lemuel Hotchkiss. They entered that mill but were soon dispersed by the local forces. The militia retaliated and fired on the invaders, killing two redcoats and taking fourteen prisoners back to the powder mill. The rest of the raiding British army marched down what is now Blake Street, and another group marched down what is now Whalley Avenue toward New Haven.

THE PIRATE OF HOTCHKISSTOWN

HAUNTED HOUSE

New Haven Register, 1901

In the town of Woodbridge, about a mile beyond the forks in the highway where stands the Harper paper mill, is the Sperry residence built full 100 years ago. It is of two stories and is said to be the only brick house in that town. The brick that entered into the walls was either from Hamden or North Haven manufacture. The farm on which the house stands at one time stood on "Sperry's Farms," and years ago there was a little settlement there. It was erected and occupied by Albert Sperry, a noted builder of his day who built the North, now United, Church in this city. The farm was owned many years ago by Richard Sperry, one of the original settlers of the town who fed and befriended the regicides. The house he occupied at one time stood on "Sperry's Farms," near the present brick structure.

In the brick house was born Peck Sperry of Woodbridge and Willis G. Miller of this city. It is one of the houses most remembered by strangers who drive through on the Litchfield Turnpike, because it is quite remarkable to see a brick residence in that neighborhood. Several ancient trees and part of the old door yard fence are still standing. The house has two chimneys and was considered one of the handsomest houses in the town at the time of its erection.

By some it bears the name of "the Haunted House." Ex-Postmaster Sperry was asked about the place yesterday, and he said:

> I doubt if it was known as the haunted house. As I remember, it was the old Wilson house that bore the reputation of having been haunted. Some 75 years ago it was said that the notorious robbers Thunderbolt and Lightfoot, as they were called, had a rendezvous in that neighborhood

and it was said that one of them hid his booty in the Wilson house. They were among the most notorious robbers in the county in their day, and as the Wilson house had this story connected with it, some timid ones later on had a sort of superstitious fear about the place. But the Sperry house was vacant for a time and it may also have gotten the reputation of being haunted, although I never heard of it. The Wilson was a stuccoed house built of brick and stone, but the Sperry house was the only purely brick house in the town.

"Is the house that was your birthplace still standing, Mr. Sperry?"

No, it was pulled down two years ago. It was in a state of almost utter collapse and although we thought a great deal of it, it had really passed all thought of repair. It was built in 1701 consequently was almost 200 years old. But after its demolition I took some masons out there and roofed over the great old chimney of stone and brick, which is still standing. There is an oven in that chimney capacious enough to take in a six foot log. I own two acres of the old homestead farm and shall keep it as long as I live. On the "Farms" once stood the original water mill that ground the corn for the colonists, and later one of the first cloth mills was erected on the site. I have in my possession one of the bricks from the chimney of my birthplace that bears the date of the year when the house was built—"1701." The house was two stories on the front and then sloped back with a linter roof like the construction of many of the houses of two centuries ago, and there are a number of such houses standing in this county today.

The Wilson house, associated with Captain Thunderbolt, still existing at 66 Bradley Road, Woodbridge, was definitely in the possession of Mr. Robert Wilson in the mid-nineteenth century. Whether he was related to Dr. John Wilson remains unknown, but Robert Wilson mysteriously vanished in 1867 and was finally claimed dead in 1902. Afterward the house passed on to his heirs, who owned it until 1966.

Captain Thunderbolt's Abode

Evening Leader, circa 1890
The Legend of a Haunted House in Woodbridge
Queer Story of Love and Cruelty
The Old Robber Chief Was the "Bogyman" of Westville and Woodbridge Sixty Years Ago—Reward for His Capture but Never Molested
"All houses wherein men have lived and died are haunted houses."
—Old Adage

There's a queer old house in Woodbridge, near the New Haven line. Its stuccoed walls can be seen from the lower road gleaming white against the purple background of West Rock.

Even to the casual observer the isolated location of the dwelling awakens curiosity, but as it is some distance from the road and only accessible through a narrow lane, it is very improbable that many give it close inspection.

This old structure, as related to this writer by an old resident, leaves much that is mysterious, and will recall to the minds of those who were youths in that vicinity sixty-nine years ago, their dreaded bogyman, "Old Thunderbolt," of whom this sketch has to do.

About 1830, it is said, the good people of Westville were stirred out of their usual routine by the appearance of an uncouth, furtive-eyed man, who engaged board near the Club House, which was then Pendleton Tavern, and gave his name as Wilson.

His queer actions and avoidance of all conversation, his sudden disappearances that lasted for months, his unexpected returns, with always plenty of money, and his unknown occupation caused much speculation among the villagers, who could not understand unsociability and secretion and must necessarily view with distrust a man who could not look them in the eyes squarely and who preferred dark byways to lighted thoroughfares at night. But in the midst of these suspicions Cupid came along and, for the want of something better to do perhaps, launched an arrow that pierced the old man's armor, to some extent at least.

Theirs must have been a queer wooing, the rosy-cheeked domestic of the boardinghouse and that silent old man who would follow her in town and out without uttering a word. Perhaps he hypnotized her, and perhaps it was his gold. Anyhow, they were married, although the girl's friends implored her to refuse him.

As would be expected, the lone dwelling near the rock just suited Wilson, which he purchased and soon went there to live with his young wife.

As time went on he became more and more eccentric. When the wife's friends called and were admitted at the front door they frequently caught glimpses of the husband's coattails disappearing at the rear.

Then stories were whispered around of dark nights when lights flickered from window to window and unearthly sounds floated from the lone dwelling. That old "Wilson" was a tyrant and a cruel one there was little doubt, as day after day in harvest time the girl wife could be seen in the field harnessed to a cart dragging the farm produce like a beast of burden driven by her lord and master. And once while enraged over some trivial thing he chased her nearly a mile with a carving knife, swearing that he would kill her, but was caught and disarmed by two men and it would have fared hard with Wilson but for the pleading of his abused wife. About this time a pamphlet offering a reward for the notorious robber chief "Captain Thunderbolt," supposed to have fled to this country after committing numerous crimes, and describing Wilson so minutely that it left little doubt in the minds of the people that he and "Thunderbolt" were one and the same person. The pamphlet also gave the dying confession of Lightfoot, a member of the robber band, telling the horrible cruelty of Thunderbolt while he (Lightfoot) was wounded in not allowing him a morsel of food for several days, saying that his wounds would heal quicker thereby. All this caused the good people to shake their heads with the usual "I told you so." But for the wife's sake they made no further investigation.

Be this as it may, old Wilson died without molestation, carrying his secret with him to the grave.

There was a man called Dr. John Wilson, born John Doherty in England in 1788, who arrived in Brattleboro, Vermont, in 1818. Wilson was believed to be Captain Thunderbolt, a notorious British highwayman who robbed his victims with lightning speed. He was known to have been a courteous thief who would not rob women. Perhaps finding a way out of his life of crime, Wilson studied medicine at the University of Edinburgh from 1815 to 1818. He fled to Dummerston, Vermont, where he practiced medicine and then designed and built a round brick schoolhouse in 1821 in Brookline, Vermont. Its round design was rumored to make it easier for him to see if authorities were coming from any direction so he could prepare and flee.

Thunderbolt's Irish partner in crime, Michael Martin, dubbed Captain Lightfoot, came to America around the same time and may have shared a space with Thunderbolt in the round schoolhouse for a few weeks until he left and continued his criminal activities. Lightfoot was captured and hanged in Cambridge, Massachusetts, in 1821. Dr. Wilson then became wary of his own capture. But his reputation in Vermont was sparkling and he was described by those in his community as a well-respected physician and liked by children. He was also known to flirt with women and drink heavily at Saturday night dances until he couldn't stand. He died in 1847.

The story of Thunderbolt and Lightfoot was turned into a Hollywood western tale in 1974, starring Clint Eastwood and Jeff Bridges.

More tales of the notorious highwayman's possible connection to the area began to surface with the following articles. Although there appears to be no correlation with the Captain Thunderbolt already mentioned, these descriptions are quite fascinating.

HOW CAPTAIN THUNDERBOLT THE FIERCE PIRATE OF 1770 TERRORIZED QUIET WESTVILLE

New Haven Union, June 22, 1913

Perhaps 'tis from the whispering wind through the tall pine trees that surround it, or is it from the murmuring brook that gives one the impression "Yo ho, ho, and a bottle of rum!" is the only singsong notes in the still woodland about the old castle in Westville wherein dwelt the dreaded Captain Jack Thunderbolt way back there in 1770. Of course you've heard that fierce old war dog of the ante-Revolutionary days, that pirate who fearlessly sailed the high seas and laughed in the face of King George II's officers when they tried to put an end to his lawlessness. The legends of this old pirate are rich with old buccaneer tales of daring and bravado, in Westville and of his unwelcome visit to that quiet little village are many.

THE OLD SEA DOG'S HOME

And the house connected with these legends is still standing. This old stone building where Captain Thunderbolt made his home and incidentally hiding place is nestled away in a shady nook on one of the slopes of West Rock, on the lower Woodbridge road, which at one time was the old stage road from New Haven to towns and villages up the Naugatuck River. It is a house that would attract the attention of the casual passerby because of its singularly odd construction. It stands some two hundred yards back from the main road directly under the towering edge of the rock. Indeed, if this gigantic piece of earth came tumbling down, it would fully cover the old time castle completely; as it is, the rock serves as a shield from the winds from the north and east. Thunderbolt's home, built of stone stuccoed gray, is the only structure of its kind in the entire valley; the door is rounded, the windows of many panes and the colonial architecture is mainly featured by the unique pillars that stretch up to the roof. There is a balcony built on the south side, so that it impresses one of the old-style Georgian buildings.

Little Known of His Life

It was in this house that Captain Thunderbolt stayed was known to the villagers he was hiding several years previous to the outbreak of the Revolutionary War. History has it that Thunderbolt, as he chose to call himself, was a well-known buccaneer and pirate whose blood-curdling deeds on the high seas had attracted the attention of the British admiralty courts and who had him forced into retirement in some secluded village. For the reputation he gained for himself in Westville during the two or three years of his life there about 1770, Captain Thunderbolt had passed through even a more lawless career than was ever recorded.

Legend never handed down his real name nor is anything definite known of his life prior to his advent into Westville, but his deeds furnished enough gossip for the village, and according to the reports he carried matters as high-handed as did Stevenson's "Billy Bones."

Westville in those days was known as Hotchkissville and was a small hamlet, and consisted of small dwellings on either side of the road from Woodbridge to Whalley Avenue and Fountain Street, and there clustered a number of old homesteads about the town tavern and public house famous as a coaching place and stage tavern. This was on the old Post Road, and was generally frequented by travelers. It is still there. The villagers were all farmers and lived quiet lives as all farmers do; and they earned a livelihood by marketing their products in New Haven.

His Arrival in Westville

Into this quiet and provincial hamlet that had never known a disturbing element, there dropped as from the mantle of the zenith in 1770 a gaudily dressed and ferocious mannered man, accompanied by two wild-looking fellows who at once took possession the village. Thunderbolt rented a house on the road running north of town and from that on for two or three years he kept the villagers on tiptoe until he left the place. Who he was or where he came from no one knew, although the village gossips at once wagged their tongues as to his past. He was a big fellow, broad of shoulder and deep of chest, and he had brawny fists, which he brought crashing down on the table in the tavern frequently to send the villagers scampering in all directions when he gave an order. He gave the name Captain Thunderbolt, and his ferocious refusal to all who inquired in his history soon made it felt that he desired his stay in Westville to be one of undisturbed quietue.

But Once Was the Buccaneer Beaten

On Saturday evenings he thundered down the country road and, spreading on a table in the village tavern a pile of gold, he drank his full till midnight. On such occasions old Thunderbolt was in a mood that brooked no interference, and when he asked a man to drink with him, 'twould be best for the man's health if he complied with the pirate's wish.

It was on such a night like this that a stranger to the ways of the village happened in on the habitués of the tavern and called for a drink of ale.

"O'd's life, man, and you will drink with me this evening," remarked Thunderbolt after eyeing the stranger closely for some time. The stranger who had noticed the bully replied quietly: "I guess I'll have my glass and be gone."

"You'll drink with me, as I live, and I want your company!" shouted the captain, while the villagers clustered at the other tables shrank in their seats in terror, expecting him to take the stranger by the coat lapel, as he had done to many a country bumpkin, and force a bottle of beer down his throat.

"As for that," replied the stranger firmly, "I say I will do nothing of the kind."

The bully was on his feet in an instant and staggered over to the stranger, grabbed his coat collar and with an oath, prepared to beat him, but was sent sprawling with a blow from the newcomer. Both whipped out their pistols and blazed away. Thunderbolt was hit and fell to the floor again, but was yanked to his feet by the stranger, who caught him by the red handkerchief that was wound about his throat and then threw him bodily into a seat.

"Now," said the stranger, "if I hear of your doing this sort of thing again I'll come back and give you the drubbing you deserve. I have heard of you before, and a word to the proper authorities may have ever a better effect."

Was Young Aaron Burr

The stranger departed after drinking his ale, while the bully sulkily finished the evening cursing and drinking. Cowed, the landlord supplied him with wine until he was very drunk. The next day the story of the encounter was village talk, and all sorts of rumors as to the identity of the man who took the bully in hand were current. A farmer from Derby, hearing the talk and the description of the young man, said: "Your visitor last night was young Burr. Aaron his name is; he has been visiting friends up my way for the past two weeks." Aaron Burr figured prominently nine years later as the leader of a regiment of volunteer colonists of Derby and Woodbridge who assisted in the repulsion of the British invading New Haven.

A Sad Romance

But Captain Thunderbolt seldom if ever met his match in the simple country folk, and for the most part carried matters in a high-handed way by his overbearing manner, and the stories of the terror is which he held of the villagers was the chatter of housewives and the food of taverns for generations afterward. Stories were told of the beer festivals at his home on the north road, which were attended by queer-looking men, for the most part from pirate ship crews. One story, which is touched with both romance and sadness, is the chief marking of his sensational stay in Westville. There was a young girl living in the center of the hamlet who was admired by all the young men, particularly one whom she had promised to wed. One day she was passing by the home of Captain Thunderbolt, and the old fellow hobbled down from his stone castle and was taken at once with her beauty, and inquired who she was. When he learned he immediately saw her father and asked permission to woo the daughter. Of course, the old farmer was taken aback by the request, yet blanched with fear when Thunderbolt demanded that it be complied with. He even named a certain day when the girl would have to be turned over to him, or he would take her by force.

The old father took ill that night and remained at the point of death for two weeks, the day appointed passing without appraising Thunderbolt's intended bride of what had transpired. So that one cool evening in June when the quietude of the little village was beautiful in a marked degree, a small band of swarthy, red-sashed, drunken sailors swaggered down the road into the town and surrounded the home of the girl while the captain smote the door with his heavy oak cane and called for the delivery of his prize. Several of the young fellows of the village got wind of what was going on, and with a band of men from this city quietly crept in on the sailors and took them completely by surprise. All but two were knocked insensible. Captain Thunderbolt held his own, however, and retreated to his castle in the woods.

But another expedition on a stormy night proved successful, Thunderbolt carried the girl in his arms to the stone house and enthroned on the big chair in his dining room, he condescended to be married to her by a parson, who was too frightened to refuse to tie the knot. Afterward, however, when the captain and his mates were drinking their fill, the minister placed a ladder against the rear of the building and up to the window of a room in which Thunderbolt's prize was a prisoner. She made good her escape but died from the shock of the affair a few months later in the home of a friend in this city.

And the End of the Legend

The captain lived for three years at the old house on the north road. He was wont to accost any farmer he met on the road into the village and capture him if he had to use a cudgel, and then bring him into the tavern and get him drunk. This condition of affairs continued until one night three strangers walked into the tavern and posted a document on the wall signed with the king's seal. When they had left, Thunderbolt pushed all the eager villagers aside and read the first lines, which told that a price was set on his head. He went white with fear when he first read it, then with an ill attempt at braggadocio ripped off the bill and ordered that none of the present inform the officers of the king that he was hiding there.

He walked out of the tavern and up the winding road between the drooping elms. That's the last time he was seen, and that's the end of the legend too.

Swashbuckling Pirate Once Terror of Westville

New Haven Register, August 19, 1928
Mysterious Captain Thunderbolt Lived in Shadow of West Rock and Went on Frequent Rampages at Old Tavern. Good Folks of Town Would Shiver with Fear Every Time Bad Man Imbibed.

"Deeds of Derring Do"

That's the old-time pirate stuff and someone has written to the Old-Timer about Captain Thunderbolt, who was our only true and never-to-be-forgotten pirate, and a very good pirate for a summer story, on the whole.

It recalls "deeds of derring do" and it smacks of bloody things and all of that bold, bad Robert Louis Stevenson stuff.

Obscure

Berkeley R. Moulthrop of Short Beach opened this little-traversed yarn about "Captain Thunderbolt," the mysterious pirate of Westville in the ante-Revolutionary days, who was the terror of Westville and who had that famous affair with Aaron Burr and hadth love as well. I had almost forgotten the tale, but with the many stories of the late Henry T. Blake of the New Haven Park Board, upon the matter and with the services of the staff of the New Haven Public Library, with what I already know about the affair, one can get a fine idea of a good old-fashioned pirate romance.

It is one of the "Yo, ho, and a bottle of rum" type.

Mr. Moulthrop writes to the Old-Timer thus:

"Can you tell us something concerning the historic old Captain Thunderbolt house which is still standing beneath the slopes of West Rock in the town of Westville?"

Fugitive

It was a stuccoed house, with tall portico pillars and was said to have been built in the eighteenth century.

It was said to have been occupied by a fugitive English pirate, who lived a retired but turbulent life, visited often by members of his crew and other outlaws.

When a proclamation describing it was hung up in the old public house tavern by the oak tree pirate appeared at once. Many stories of old orgies and even murder were concerned with the early history of this house.

Mr. Moulthrop is right in his outline of this famous old story, which has to do with one of the oldest and most picturesque of New Haven's environments. It was a hummer here in the seventeen hundreds. Of course we all know the story of the regicides, but the tale of the retired pirate is not familiar "by us," as the Dutchman did remark. However, local legend is rich with stories of the old buccaneer, Captain Thunderbolt; and, by the way, nobody has ever been found who can give his other name.

But the stories of bravado and daring of the unwelcome visitor were many.

House

His old house still stands on the slopes of West Rock, on what is known as the lower Woodbridge road. It is a house that would attract attention from anyone, because of its novel construction. Substantially built of stone and stuccoed all over, a dull gray, it has the small windowpanes of the old days. But the unique feature of the house is the pillars and balcony that run along half of the southern side.

In this house, Captain Thunderbolt, as he was known and dreaded by the villagers, lived in hiding for several years previous to the outbreak of the Revolutionary War. He was a well-known English pirate and buccaneer whose bloodthirsty deeds on the high seas had attracted the attention of the

British admiralty courts, and who had been forced into retirement in some secluded village while the hue and cry for his capture was carried on in the largest seaports.

From the character that he had gained for himself during three or four years of his life there, about 1770, it was seen that Captain Thunderbolt was a man who had passed through a most lawless career. He carried matters there with high hand.

Rum

In those days the village rum hole was "The Tavern" at Whalley Avenue and Fountain Street, which inn I regret to say has been torn down within a few years. This was an inn that was largely patronized by travelers up through the Naugatuck Valley from New Haven.

Into this pastoral element there fitted in Captain Thunderbolt, red-sashed and domineering with two wild-looking seamen. He was a big man, and made such a big noise about the place that the Westvillites quickly left him alone. Nothing of importance except liquor was heard of him after he had once become ensconced in the stuccoed house alluded to above.

Coin

Once a week, on Saturday evenings, he would thunder down the country road to the tavern at Fountain Street, spread a bag of coin of all sorts of denominations on one of the tavern tables and drink his fill until midnight. On such occasions he was generally in a mood that brooked little or no interference, although occasionally he would break out into a sort of lion-like generosity, when it would be worth a man's life—the Westvillites believed to refuse his drinks.

The gentle reader will recollect that prohibition was not in effect at that time.

Burr

On one of these nights a stranger from up the Derby road dropped in and bought a glass of nut brown ale from local stock. He was a likely looking young man and Captain Thunderbolt finally shot out at him:

"Od's life, man, you will drink with me, this evening."

The stranger, who had not noticed the bronzed old pirate before, declined with thanks. He would drink his own glass and be gone.

"I say you will drink with me and as long as I want your [expletive] company," shouted the captain while the villagers at the other end of the table shrank into their seats with terror, expecting to see him take the stranger by the coat lapel, as he had done to more than one country bumpkin, and force a bottle of liquor down his throat.

"As to that," said the stranger quietly, "I'll do nothing of the kind."

The bully started for the young man but in a moment the stranger sent the sailor sprawling with a fist blow and both men then pulled pistols and blazed away at each other. The stranger finally winged the sailor and left him in a heap on the floor, calling him down for being a bully.

He warned him against a reputation of such tactics in a civilized Yankee community.

Later it was learned that the stranger who "trimmed" Captain Thunderbolt was none the less than Aaron Burr, who figured nine years later as the leader of the Derby troops when they flocked into New Haven to repel the British invasion.

Rowdy

Thus Captain Thunderbolt. He was a rowdy of the first class. While he was hanging about Westville he became enamored of a farmer's daughter, who is said to have been unusually beautiful (they all are, you know), and whom sought to carry. She refused him and he brought some of his men to kidnap the girl. Young bloods of Westville beat him out, however, and he was defeated.

On a second attempt he was more successful and he forced a weak-kneed local dominie to marry him to the girl. She escaped by means of a ladder. The fright of the evening's experience was too much for her, however, and she died in the house of a friend in New Haven soon after.

Pistol

After this Thunderbolt became more domineering than ever. He carried a huge horse pistol, which he was accustomed to discharge into crowds, and he would drag any of the dwellers of the village into the tavern to drink with him whenever he chose.

Terror

Just who this terror of the village was, no one seems to have discovered until the incident occurred that rid the village of the captain and unfolded the mystery.

Those were the days of privateering on the high seas by sailors both of the colonies and of England, and the ocean and inlets along the coast were also the stamping ground of hundreds of pirates who plundered and killed to their fill all along the shores.

Commissions were sent out for the heads of scores of these buccaneers and it only needed identification to secure the trial and hanging of any one of the numerous fugitives for whom the open main had become too warm a place.

Three or four times a year Captain Thunderbolt was visited by a crew of swarthy seamen, black faced and swaggering, with the particular roll of the sailor. These bands came always at night over land from some cove along the shore, and their visits always coincided with the appearance on the Sound of some low, long English vessel that flew that flag and then audaciously ran up the black flag when putting out from shore. These fellows always bore with them a bag or a box that was heavily loaded with all kinds of material, and after they had gone, the captain had "money to burn" for several months.

But the day of trouble finally came to Captain Thunderbolt. One day a couple of king's officials came into the Westville tavern where the captain was drinking and nailed a notice up on the wall, which held the king's commission for his head. And on the notice his atrocities were named. He was one of the fugitive pirate captains.

England was looking for him and a slip noose was waiting in port of the English domains. All of the villagers gathered about the bill but the captain thrust them all to one side so that he could read it first. The initial sentence

It is revealed that the feared Captain Thunderbolt used to frequent the large building at the left of this circa 1908 postcard view. West up Whalley Avenue at the junction of Fountain Street is the town tavern, later named the Elm House. The stucco-covered stone building was built in the mid-seventeenth century and was the main gathering place in town until it was torn down around 1910. *Courtesy of Joseph Taylor.*

brought the old villain up with a jerk. He turned as weak as a cat and called for his cane. Turning to the room full he said with his old-time swagger and bravado of voice: "If any blank blank of you speaks of this afore I leaves this blank blank town I'll blow his blank blank head off."

With that he ripped down the bill, jammed it into his pocket, gathered his goods together and sailed out of Milford Harbor and Westville was rid of his terror for all time.

Where he went or whatever became of him, history does not record, but he probably, like others of his compatriots, was swung at the end of a yard arm by some judicial sea lawyer as a windup to a bloody career.

The saloon where Captain Thunderbolt was said to have frequented was the old Elm House that once existed at the fork where Whalley Avenue and Fountain Street intersect.

THE WESTVILLE TAVERN

circa 1908

Before long the Westville Tavern at the junction of Fountain Street and Whalley Avenue will be torn down to give way for a monument to be erected to the founder of the Greist Manufacturing Company, donated by the members of his family. This ancient hostelry goes back farther than the memory of any living resident of Westville, back to the days of the War of 1812. It always has been a public gathering place, first being an ale house and hotel.

Old Charlie Morse was the proprietor back in the forties. When he died his widow, whom everyone knew as "Mrs. Morse," continued to run the house until war days. Some of the older men in Westville, men well past the half-century mark, remember Mrs. Morse very well and also chuckle over the tricks they delighted in playing on her and in which she seemed to take an interest even when most severe apparently. It was suspected that she had a warm place in her heart for all boys.

After Mrs. Morse was running the place alone, the tavern became famous for its dinners and its fine cooking. It was a favorite mecca for those who went driving or walking and any evening parties of New Haven people might be found having a quiet dinner in one of the rooms, low ceilinged, dark and antique in furnishings.

William Scoville succeeded Mrs. Morse and he ran a general store in connection with the bar and lodging facilities. He in turn was followed by Sereno Wilson, he again by William H. Peck and then Mrs. Morse, when growing feeble, sold the tavern to J.A. Hatch, who ran it until bought out by John Tyler.

The Westville Tavern always has been the gathering place of the clans—political. Here deals were made and put through whenever possible. Here the Edgewood dopesters are "figgering" on election probabilities and possibilities.

Nothing very exciting, no spectacular things, happened at the Tavern but this routine was unusual and the characters who frequent the place were the kind who appear now only in olden stories. An ancient Westville institution is dying. It has been outgrown. The tavern is no longer a necessity or indeed a convenience. Other things and other manners have taken the place of life in the ancient tavern as it was partially known to the men who were boys in Westville.

INDUSTRY, INVENTIONS, FIRES AND FLOODS

Westville was a hamlet of industry built along the West River and two smaller streams. Since its founding, mills were built to grind corn and make paper, cloth, dyes, matches, cutlery, tools, machines and other instruments of trade. Over the years, fires and floods have plagued the town's manufacturing sites.

Some of the earliest mills in New Haven were built along the West River behind Valley Street. Captain John Munson, along with members of the Hotchkiss family, ran a gristmill on the West River by the mid-eighteenth century. Nearby, Joseph Mix ran a gristmill until 1775 and sold the land in 1768 to Joseph Munson, a prominent landowner in Westville. In 1786, Munson sold the property to Elijah Thomson.

One of the earliest photographic views of Westville, this image shows the town from the estate of Donald Grant Mitchell on Forest Road in 1869. The pastoral scene shows a snippet of life in Westville but it can't show the fires, collisions and flood events that changed the landscape and tested its citizens. *Photographed by Rockwood. Courtesy of Colin M. Caplan.*

Elijah Thompson was an influential man in Connecticut and his family owned considerable land along the West River and in Westville. He fought with the Second Company in the Revolutionary War. His strong will helped him get rid of his tobacco habit for a while when he put his tobacco into a box and sent it down the West River. When one of his farmhands found the box of tobacco floating in the river and returned it to Mr. Thompson, he believed that divine Providence had caused this to happen, allowing him to enjoy this vice. In his will, Mr. Thompson set aside land for a town farm in Westville for the almshouse and a tract of land was given to the Asylum for the Insane in Hartford.

WESTVILLE MILLS, ETC.

The Attractions of New Haven, Connecticut, 1869
By S.H. Elliot

Westville lies within the township of New Haven; only a small part of the village is within the limits of the city. It is but two miles from the center of the city, and there are some extensive business establishments in the place, well worth the time to see, speak of and to visit. For instance, there is the hardware casting and furnace works of the Blake Brothers on Blake Street, a house long established, universally known and esteemed. Not dealing in exact figures, we should say in general, their house had a name and existence equally long with the Harpers' in New York, and like that, wherever known, held in the highest regard. They employ a large force of hands and carry out a course as thorough in their business as discipline in the army. They have gone through pressure in the market, fire and have even had laid on them the touch of the finger of death; and still the house moves on steady and calm, fulfilling its ends. Two of their celebrated inventions are these: the little hickory nut cracker and the huge stone crusher for macadamized roads. They have maintained their right in this patent against suits in this country, and we think in Europe. Then we come to the extensive Beecher Basket Works and Friction Matches of A. Beecher and sons. They employ a large number of hands and turn off an incredible amount of work. Indeed, enormous quantities of these baskets (saying nothing of the match boxes and other work) are here manufactured and carted off as freight to many different points. The extent to which this business has grown is truly wonderful. More than a million strawberry baskets are made annually. The Hardware and Manilla Paper Mill, right at the foot of the West Rock ledge, is worth going over. Mr. Peck, the former owner, has left it in the hands of Mr. A.B. Mallory, and under his charge the works are throwing off a great quantity of the best wrapping paper in market. Then there are the extensive works of Mr. E. Merriman on the other side of the stream, nearer the base of West Rock. Just above these works is the heavy and well known Paper Mill of Messrs. Fred. & Jos. Parker. Their extensive range of machinery enables them to prepare almost any style of paper that is in demand and to seize every opportunity that the state of trade permits to improve their instruments.

As not long since, we found they were all shut down on newspapers and were running day and night on the first quality of heavy paper for neck collars. They employ a great many women in the rag department and give work to a large class of villagers and to hands from abroad. Their works are run at great expense and we hope with corresponding profit.

Farther up the stream, we come to the paper mill and works of James Harper, called the Lilly Pond Paper Mill. This mill has in hand the supply of large orders of *news* paper. It makes large shipments to New York and elsewhere, manufacturing a very superior paper at fair prices. All these works lie along close under the brows of West Rock and are all within distance of a mile. At Westville the "Elm City" laundry is established, and may be said to be now a necessity to New Haven. This company is driven hard to perform its weekly engagements. Its teams course the city at all hours of the day gathering up parcels or returning the clean and shining linen to the different owners. The churches and schools of Westville, the post offices, stores, all lie near together, and the city of New Haven is accessible to the whole by a few moments' ride in the horse cars.

The first paper mill in New Haven was located on the West River near Valley Street in 1776 when Joseph Munson sold the land and water rights to Lemuel Hotchkiss and five partners for the purpose of a paper mill. In 1789, Abel Buell, a well-known silversmith who established a mint in New Haven, began a cotton mill along the West River south of Valley Street. He partnered with William McIntosh from Scotland. The General Assembly granted them a $3,000 subsidy because it was one of the first cotton mills in America. The mill also began calico printing on the cloth and later produced woolen cloth and paper. That mill burned in 1836 and was replaced by another paper mill in 1840, called the West Rock Paper Mill. It was built by Joseph Parker, who pioneered the use of cotton waste from cotton mills to produce the first fine book paper in the country. Mr. Parker's brother,

Frederick S. Parker, joined the firm in 1841, which then became the F.S. & J. Parker & Company. They began to manufacture blotting paper in 1859. Soon after they became the country's largest producer of blotting paper and exported their Treasury Blotting Paper around the world.

    Blake Brothers, partnered by Eli Whitney Blake and his brothers Philos P. and John A., began its door hardware company on the corner of Fitch and Blake Streets in 1830. It was the first firm in the country to manufacture mortised door locks, in 1835, and in 1838 it patented casters for stowaway beds. Philos P. Blake eventually invented the corkscrew in 1860.

    Anson Beecher moved to New Haven in 1853 and began the A. Beecher & Sons match manufacturers at the rear of 200 Valley Street. He invented five machines that assisted in the manufacturing of the first phosphorus parlor matches. He then combined to make the Swift, Courtney & Beecher Company in 1870. In 1881, it became the Diamond Match Company, one of the largest match operations in the country. Anson's son, L. Wheeler, joined him in the original company until he began the Geometric Tool Co. on the site of the Diamond Match Company.

STILL ANOTHER FIRE

Columbian Register, December 31, 1842

On Thursday evening, about eight o'clock, a fire broke out in the large wooden building in Westville, known as the "Bunce Paper Mill," which was entirely destroyed. There was a thick snow raging at the time, which prevented the fire itself from being visible, although the heavens in that direction were of a bright red glow. The engines were turned out, but the general supposition being that it was only the Northern Lights they returned and it was not generally known until Friday morning, in the city, that there had actually been a fire. We understand that the property was insured $2,000. It was occupied by Mr. Lyman Church for the manufacture of wrapping paper, a large quantity of which was on hand. The fire caught in the bleaching room and so rapid was its progress that two young men who were present had barely time to escape.

    The singular appearance of the heavens caused many very worthy old ladies in the city to believe that the fulfillment of Miller's prophecies was

Lemuel Hotchkiss built this old paper mill, the first of its kind in New Haven, in 1776 along the banks of the West River. The dirt lane on the left-hand side is Valley Street and the cliffs of West Rock soar in the background. The mill was the scene of a fiery inferno on the night of December 29, 1842. This scene was drawn and painted around 1825. *Painted by John Rubens Smith. Courtesy of the Library of Congress.*

even at their doors. A wicked wag of a horseman galloped through Chapel Street, crying out at the top of his lungs that "the world was on fire," and the audience at a religious meeting was gravely cautioned as to the probable nature of the phenomenon. We understand that Mr. Greeley pronounced it "quite unaccountable"—and unless he was correctly informed before he left the city, we may expect a scientific dissertation in the next *Tribune* on the "Age of Miracles Returned"—What with meteors, shooting stars, blue fish and "unaccountable phenomenon," New Haven is getting to be a settlement of some note in the world.

The following article also covers the fire at the Bunce Paper Mill on December 29, 1842.

THE MILLERITE DELUSION

Outline History of New Haven, 1884
By Henry Howe

The Millerite Delusion was rife at this period, when it was predicted the world was to come to an end.

On the night of December 20, 1842, during a heavy snowstorm, the whole heavens were aglow with a mysterious lurid light, and the believers hereabouts felt that the end of all things was at hand; and multitudes of others who had not before believed were filled with awe.

The firemen were not so badly scared but they were able to get out their machines, and one company had dragged theirs up as far as the head of Broadway when they were stopped by an old gentleman, a fervent Millerite and Methodist exhorter, who exclaimed: "Go back with your machine, young men! This is a fire all the water in the world can never quench, for the Lord God Almighty is now coming in all his glory!" The next morning the tidings came to town that Bunce's paper mill, out in Westville, had been burned the night before.

Living out on Orange Street in a little house at this time was "Black Milly," an eccentric colored woman known to everyone in town, as her occupation of peddling yeast made from hops, or as it was anciently called, "emptyins," which she drew in a little hand cart from door to door. Everyone smiled when her name was mentioned. The sharp or odd things that fell from her lips, and her comical performances and vociferous shoutings at Methodist meetings, had made her locally famous. Next morning she was called upon by a neighbor, when she said: "O you ought to have seen me last night. How happy I was! I thought my blessed Jesus was coming. Then I got up and trimmed my lamps and set them a'burning, and put my house in order, and sat here waiting to give him a welcome." Milly was a good woman and, living an upright life, could not fail of being respected.

STORM AND FRESHET

New Haven Palladium, March 29, 1843

The severe storm, first of snow and then of rain, on Monday and Tuesday proves to have been very disastrous to the roads and bridges in this section of the state, especially in this county. The Fair Haven bridge has been damaged at the west end, and several bridges have been carried away on Mill River—also the West Bridge on the New York turnpike, a bridge on the Derby road and one at Whitneyville, and another at Westville, & c. and worse than all, we regret to hear of a loss of life at Westville. Mr. Orville Collins, firm of A. Collins & Son of Straitsville, in attempting to cross the bridge (near Bradley's Spring Factory in Westville) that, as well as the road, was covered with water, mistook the path and drove into the stream, and he and his two horses were drowned. A companion in the wagon with him escaped. Mr. Collins leaves a wife and five children to deplore his untimely end.

All the land mails of yesterday, except those by railroad, were brought back to the post office, as it was impossible for them to proceed.

The canal is but little damaged as far as heard from. We learn that the flood was not severe in Hartford.

Due to this damaging flood, the old wooden bridge dating to the establishment of the Litchfield Turnpike around 1800 was replaced with a new stone arch bridge built on Whalley Avenue across the West River. The builder, Edward Hine of Woodbridge, promised that this bridge would be indestructible. That was an overstatement because on October 4, 1869, the stone bridge was swept away. It took months to plan and rebuild a new bridge here. It wasn't until March 1870 that any progress was reported.

Westville Bridge

New Haven Palladium, March 28, 1870

The new Westville bridge begins to loom up, to the joy of the villagers and the persons who have to pass there in teams. The ironwork has been commenced and will be pushed ahead as rapidly as the combined efforts of the contractors and Town Agent Shelton can make it.

A more detailed description of the bridge was reported in the report of the City of New Haven.

WEST RIVER BRIDGE

City Year Book of New Haven, 1870

The new bridge built at Westville is one hundred feet long in the clear, between abutments, and sixty-six feet wide, the full width of the street; it is supported by six heavy trusses with iron beams and girders, making it an entire iron structure; the planking being the only woodwork about it. I doubt if there is a bridge in New England stronger or more substantially built. The foundations for the abutments are thickly piled, cut off and capped below the bed of the stream, which will prevent any freshet ever undermining the foundation. It is a deck bridge, with no obstructions on top, leaving a clear roadway of forty-two feet in width and a walk on each side twelve feet wide.

The calm winter scene along the banks of the West River near Valley Street was photographed on December 15, 1907. It certainly hides the fact that this river repeatedly breached its banks throughout its history, washing away bridges and mills. Some of the largest flood events on record occurred on April 28, 1842; October 4, 1869; and more recently in 1982. *Photographed by T.S. Bronson. Courtesy of the New Haven Museum & Historical Society.*

Winter freshets, or floods, usually occurred in March after a major snow melt. Water from the uplands, taking course along the West River and Wintergreen Brook, would eventually meet at Westville, where the convergence and force caused many a bridge to fail. New Haven's only waterfall, Wintergreen Falls, located at the border of Hamden, was photographed during high water around 1875. *Photographed by Charles A. Gulliver. Courtesy of Colin M. Caplan.*

The table showing the cost of the structure will give you the details of each item in its construction.

Bridges were not the only structures that needed repair and replacement. Whalley Avenue, stretching from the West River up the slope toward New Haven, became a muddy path riddled with ruts. To solve this problem, inventor Eli Whitney Blake took stone from West Rock and turned it into the macadam, or paving material. The first application of this method for road building was tested on Whalley Avenue in 1852. After the demand for this technique became widely used across the city, Blake developed a machine called the Blake Stone Breaker to crush the stone in 1857 and established it in 1868 on Springside Avenue across from the terminus of West Rock ridge. His invention went into use over the entire world for road paving and mining operations.

Incendiary Fire in Westville

New Haven Palladium, March 23, 1861
"The Malleable Iron-Works Destroyed"

At about twelve o'clock Monday night, the Malleable Iron-Works, situated near Fitch's Pond on Fitch Street, Westville, and belonging to W. & E.T. Fitch, of this city, were discovered to be on fire. The light was seen in this city, and the firemen came out generally, but after the steamer had run out some distance on Broadway, the light still appearing to be in the distance, and it being almost impossible to get on through the drifts of snow, all came back. There were, in consequence, no engines on hand, and the Works were totally destroyed.

The buildings, three in number, were 150 by 50, 100 by 30 and 75 by 30 feet in dimensions, and the loss is some $12,000, covered by insurance. Their patterns were housed in a brick safe of their own building and escaped destruction. Otherwise the loss would have been much heavier. The fire took in the rolling room, where there had been no fire this winter, and was undoubtedly the work of an incendiary. Some fifty men have been employed there, who will thus be thrown out of employment.

A couple of lads dangle their feet above the ruins of the old Blake Brothers Manufacturing Company on Blake Street near Fitch Street on December 2, 1906. The little dam here was part of the mill works that utilized little Beaver Brook. *Photographed by T.S. Bronson. Courtesy of the New Haven Museum & Historical Society.*

The loss does not in any way interfere with their carriage spring and padlock factory on East Street, which will continue operations as heretofore.

The Geometric Tool Company

This Week in New Haven, 1926

It might fittingly be said that the Geometric Tool Company, of New Haven, Connecticut, is a concern that has been threading its way through the world for the past thirty-three years. Probably no other line of manufacture enters into more products than does the cutting of screw threads.

The Geometric Tool Company, under the name of the Geometric Drill Company, started business in New Haven in 1893, in the old English building at the corner of Chapel and State Streets, and which was torn down when the railroad cut was built.

Tools for threading bicycle parts were the first contribution that the Geometric Tool Company made to quantity production. These were followed by tools for cutting the threads on various parts of agricultural machines, motors and engines, carriages, sewing machines, electrical accessories, automobile parts, motorcycles, washing machines, bread mixers, food choppers, engineering specialties, plumbers' supplies, airplanes, radio, optical supplies, surgical instruments—nearly every manufactured product of metal construction, whether for the saving of labor, for pleasure or for profit, has in its construction one or many threaded parts. When one stops to consider the vast uses to which threads are put in present-day manufacture, one can appreciate the contribution that the first manufacturers of automatic die heads and collapsing taps made to the advancement of manufacturing art. The Geometric Tool Company was one of the very first.

Many interesting records of thread cutting have been made with Geometric thread cutting tools. The mention of a few here will give some idea of the enormous manufacturing production that is represented in the one item of screw threads alone:

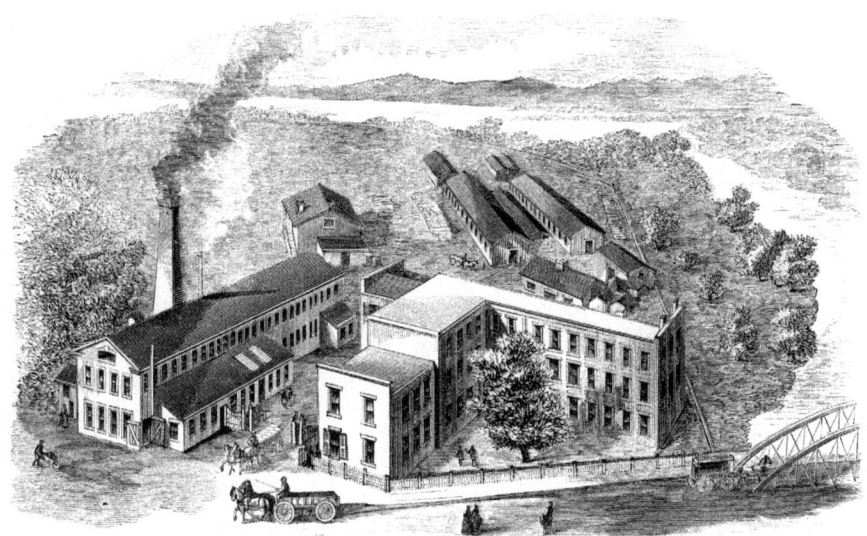

The buildings of the Swift & Courtney & Beecher Company, match makers, are shown in this woodcut from circa 1872. Here at the corner of Blake and Valley Streets on December 29, 1842, the Bunce Paper Mill burned in a huge fire. The fire was so big, lighting up the snowy sky, that a group of apocalyptic Millerites, convinced that it was the end of the world, blocked the firemen from getting to the fire. *Courtesy of Colin M. Caplan.*

The newly constructed factory and office building of the Geometric Tool Company on Valley Street shimmered in the old millpond around 1908. The pond was created in 1776 in conjunction with a paper mill, the first in New Haven. The pond was eventually filled in to create more factory space in 1912. *Photographed by T.S. Bronson. Courtesy of the New Haven Museum & Historical Society.*

An automobile concern is cutting 1,200 threads per hour on the filler and filler cap for its automobile gasoline tank. That is, 600 of the fillers and filler caps each are threaded per hour. A lamp concern is cutting 900 threads per hour on lamp parts. Another concern, 720 threads an hour on pipe nipples. On a piece calling for a thread of small diameter, 40 a minute are threaded.

The present site of the Geometric Tool Company, "under the sheltering cliffs of West Rock," has long been used for manufacturing. More than sixty years ago, Anson Beecher made baskets in the Blake Street building of the Geometric factories. His company went by the name of the Beecher Basket Company. Later the same building was used by Anson Beecher & Sons Co. for the manufacture of matches. This business was consolidated with Swift & Courtney Company of Wilmington, Delaware, and became the Swift & Courtney and Beecher Company. This company was later absorbed by the Diamond Match Company, which took the business to Barberton, Ohio.

The four Beecher sons continued to occupy the old building and maintained offices there until, one by one, death claimed them. They were public-spirited citizens and some of the important industries of New Haven owe their beginning to the guiding hand of these men. One of the enterprises that

Ebenezer Beecher supported was the Geometric Drill Company, which was later reorganized under its present name. Its growth from that time is a well-known chapter in the history of Connecticut industry. Geometric opening die heads and collapsing taps are known in all parts of the civilized world where thread cutting on any scale worth mentioning is done.

NATION'S SEWING MACHINE FITTINGS PRODUCED HERE

New Haven Evening Register, April 1929

In New Haven is situated the only plant manufacturing sewing machine attachments in the United States. Whenever women here take out their sewing machines and engage in making their own and their families' spring or winter wardrobes, no matter what make machine they use, the rufflers, hemmers, braiders and other accessories are products of the Greist Manufacturing Company.

This industry is not one of those founded in New Haven. It was begun originally in Chicago by John Milton Greist in 1871. Mr. Greist was one of the earliest inventors of attachments for sewing machines. Prior to the time when he first began manufacturing them, sewing machines could do little else than sew straight seams. All the ruffling, tucking, gathering and braiding that was so fashionable on women's garments in the mauve decade had to be sewed by hand. The machine was not then equipped with any labor- and time-saving devices as it is today.

At that time, when a woman bought a sewing machine whatever attachments she wanted, she had to purchase extra. A machine did not come fully equipped. It was not until 1889 that sewing machine companies adopted the policy of selling the attachments with the machines under one price.

In those years there were other manufacturers of sewing machine attachments. Dr. E.J. Toof was putting them out on a small scale in New Haven, and there were several other plants scattered throughout the United States.

Mr. Greist moved from Chicago to New Jersey, where he stayed only a short time. In 1890, he came to New Haven and started an assembling plant on Court Street. In 1892, encouraged by E.B. Beecher, match machinery inventor and manufacturer of the Beecher Matches, he purchased the old Clark Bit Factory in Blake Street. At the time of the purchase the building was a three-story structure with only twenty-five thousand square feet of floor space.

During the years that followed, the company, which was now incorporated as Greist Manufacturing Company, gradually acquired the attachment business of all sewing machinery manufacturers and had in the meantime bought out the interests of three other competitors, including Toof Company of this city, the Johnston Ruffler Company of Ottomwa, Iowa, and Winslow R. Parsons Company of Chicago, Illinois.

As did many other New England plants, the factory manufactured small munitions for the government during the years of the World War and at the time of the Armistice 750 men and women were employed in the Greist plants, including those working in two overflow buildings. Approximately 80 percent of the work turned out then was munitions.

Since the war, other lines have been introduced in order to utilize the increased facilities of the concern. These include the production of portable clamping electric lamps for reading and drop wires for weaving, used in the textile industry.

Because of the precision quality of the business, the Greist Manufacturing Company has been able to take orders for the manufacture of complicated mechanisms on the contract basis, among these being the manufacture of a paper cup–making machine.

The plans now cover 125,000 feet of floor space and there are four separate buildings. Sewing machine attachments are made for the White, Singer, New Home, Free, National, William & Gibbs and Standard sewing machine companies and, because each machine requires attachments in proportion to fit each standard type, much of the work is of the highly specialized type. The work itself does not call for specially designed machinery but the tools and dies are all made in the tool department maintained by the company and the most able die makers are required.

At the present time three hundred men and women are employed and practically all of the work is skilled. Mrs. J.M. Greist is president of the concern and W.C. Greist vice-president and treasurer.

LIFE IN WESTVILLE

WESTVILLE FORTY-FIVE YEARS AGO, RECALLED BY A FORMER RESIDENT

New Haven Evening Register, February 6, 1915

A man who forty-five years ago was a resident of Westville returned for a visit to his former home recently and was led to express great astonishment at the wonderful changes apparent since his departure. Especially did he note the changes in the business department. In reviewing Westville as he used to know it, he brought out many facts that are entirely new to many and almost forgotten by some of the older residents.

Speaking of Westville forty-five years ago, he said:

> It was not called Whalley Avenue in those days, it was Main Street; and Harrison Street was called Franklin Street. The changes in the names were made after Westville became a part of New Haven. Beecher Park presented a vastly different appearance at that time. On it were a number of dwellings, the "long building" and a meat market. This long building was originally the old Methodist meetinghouse. It stood on the site of the present Methodist church, but faced toward the east instead of the south. It was sold in 1853 and moved to what is now Beecher Park and used for tenements. The dwellings which stood on Beecher Park together with the long building and the market were either torn down or moved away. The market is now used by the West Rock Social club as their clubrooms. The late E.B. Beecher bought the property, filled it in and graded it, making it present the attractive appearance it does today. Of course during his lifetime it was private property and what is now the Mitchell Library was his home. Thousands of dollars were spent on this property and it was one of the finest showplaces in this part of the country.

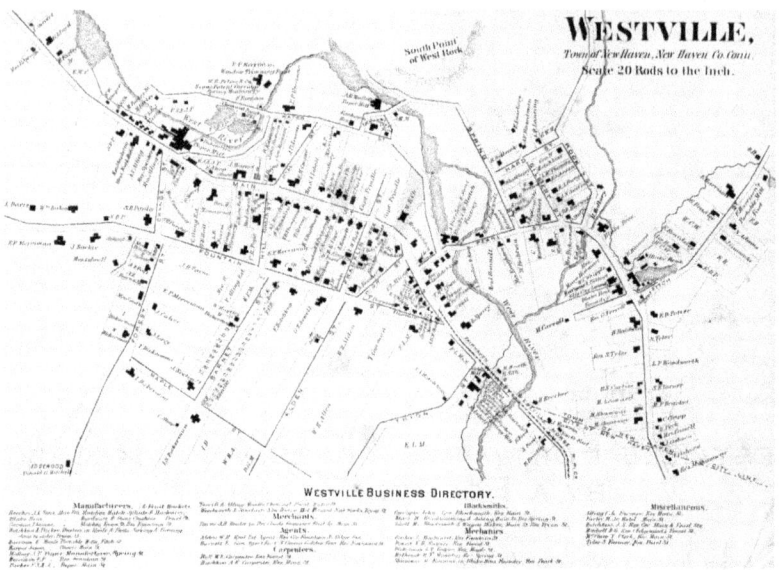

Nothing covers more ground with more information than this 1868 map of Westville. Every property owner is mentioned and their houses, factories and stores are drawn with near accurate representation. The town was divided into three school districts: west, middle and east. In 1870, when a new school was built next to the Methodist church on Whalley Avenue, the other schools were closed, and two of them moved to other locations. *Drawn by F.W. Beers. Courtesy of Colin M. Caplan.*

The view of Westville from West Rock captures the small-town feeling that separated it from nearby New Haven in the background. Westville became industrialized prior to this 1907 view, but its major residential boom was just a few years away. The old factories that can be seen in the middle of the photo grew and eventually spanned to the banks of the bordering streams. *Courtesy of Joseph Taylor.*

Philip Street, or High Street, as it was then called, was not much used; instead of coming straight down as it does now, it switched around between the Alling residence and the present post office. Another old landmark since gone out of existence was the slaughterhouse owned by Lyman Alling. It stood on the bank in back of the present post office. The Alling home looks very much the same as it did in those days, aside from the improvements made on it. The tailor shop occupied by J. Rogdanoff was formerly used as a tailor shop by A.C. Sperry. Mr. Sperry's home next door, which is an old dwelling, would not be recognized at first glance on account of the storefronts which have been added to it.

Pythian hall replaced the old Masonic hall which was burned thirty odd years ago. The first Masonic hall was a two-story building with a store on the ground floor and a hall and lodge rooms overhead; it was not nearly as large as the present structure. The store formerly occupied by Merwin's drug shop was not built at that time. The next dwelling often spoken of as the old Crandall place is perhaps the only building in the section which remains so nearly in its original state. Where the Sperry block has been erected was the site of a grocery store and a livery stable. Part of the old Franklin hall was used in the building of the Sperry block.

The opening of Central Avenue from Fountain Street to Whalley Avenue is of very recent date. In former days there was an alleyway between the store and the livery stable. The tavern or the Morse place as it was then called was an old, old landmark. Aaron Burr slept in it one night. It was torn down about five years ago. The grounds around the Mix place have undergone numerous changes, but the quaint looking old house remains exteriorly about the same.

In the early '40s, Benjamin Bradley kept a bark mill for tanning hides on the corner of Tryon's road, as it was then called. This shop was afterward used by Morris Isbell for his wagon shop. Sheldon Hotchkiss had a sash and blind shop at the corner of Whalley Avenue and Tryon Street. Both these shops were destroyed by fire and Isbell rebuilt on the New Haven side of the bridge; his shop was torn down very recently.

The West River bridge, built in 1871, replaced an old stone bridge with three arches. The stone bridge was built in 1842 by Edward Hine, a mason from Woodbridge. He said the bridge would last for all times, but it went away in a terrible freshet in October 1869. The freshet was precipitated by the giving way of the dam at the Pond Lily Dye works. The old cap stones are used as approaches to the present bridge.

On the site of the well-known Gorman Match factory, which furnished employment to so many of the older residents and was burned down about thirty-six years ago, now stands the Forsythe Dyeing Company's splendid new plant.

The drinking fountain at the junction of Whalley and Fountain Street was given by the late Mrs. Ford of Valley Street, who willed $500 for it. It replaced the iron trough put there by the city and that in turn replaced an old wooden trough and a pump. Each man got out and pumped the water for his animals to drink.

Starting from the bridge on the north side, an old blacksmith shop with a hall overhead has since been converted into a dwelling house. Tryon Street has recently been extended from Whalley to the river. Enos Sperry had a grocery store about where the present dry goods emporium now stands, and his own residence was one of the showplaces of his times; it has since been remodeled and turned into the hotel owned by Hugh McGowan. The old Hull place, which stood on the site where John Tyler's brick house now is, was originally where Enos Sperry's home stood. He moved it off to build a more pretentious residence.

It is not many years ago since John Tyler moved the brick house across the avenue. A small wooden dwelling, which stood next has since been moved up Whalley Avenue by Mrs. Mary Fitzgerald. The horse car barns, which have been razed to the ground, were built about forty years ago. The house, another very old landmark, which stood next to the barns has been razed also. Taylor's Quality Store is of more recent build, but the barbershop next to it is a very old place and was formerly the post office. That was before there were either carriers or rural delivery.

James G. Hotchkiss's residence which stood at the corner of Whalley and Blake Street has been moved down Blake to make room for the Masonic Temple. The temple is built with stores on the ground floor. One of them is occupied by F.J. Markle and another Merwin's Drug Shop, a large dance hall and lodge rooms cover the second floor. The building now occupied by Mansfield's market and the Edgewood Pharmacy was in former years Lyman Alling's dwelling.

In 1848, Eli Barnett and twelve other leaders formed a civic improvement committee. At a May 11 meeting they called for the renaming of a number of streets. The following are the streets that were changed: Whalley Avenue, originally called Litchfield Turnpike, was renamed Main Street; Fountain Street, originally called Raymond Falls Turnpike, was renamed Broad Street; Ramsdell Avenue was called West Street; Forest Road was called Orange Street; Dayton Street was also called Orange Street but was also named

Westville's Main Street allowed the town to be self-sustaining while attracting travelers from all over. This circa 1905 postcard view looking west from present Whalley and Central Avenues shows a number of local businesses, including the Hotel Edgewood on the left-hand side and the Knights of Pythias Hall, the tall building in the middle. *Courtesy of Joseph Taylor.*

Central Westville was the scene of mostly quiet and common activities. Between the factory whistles and church bells, the clap of horseshoes announced coming visitors. This scene is looking east down Whalley Avenue from the corner of Blake Street on January 24, 1908. *Photographed by T.S. Bronson. Courtesy of the New Haven Museum & Historical Society.*

This postcard view from 1908 shows the Westville Congregational Church, built in 1835 on Harrison Street. This was Westville's oldest church and the parish was organized in 1832; prior to that, churchgoers were forced to attend services on the Green in New Haven. The church's design is similar to Congregational churches built in other Connecticut towns, including Ridgefield and the Mount Carmel section of Hamden. *Courtesy of Joseph Taylor.*

Narrow Lane; West Elm Street, originally called Dickerman Lane, was renamed Maple Street; Harrison Street was called Franklin Street; Emerson Street was called Hill Street; Philip Street was called High Street and later renamed Spring Alley; Valley Street was called Water Street and later renamed Mechanic Street; West Rock Avenue, for half a block, and Central Avenue were called South Street, later renamed Tryon Street; Blake Street, originally called Town Street, was renamed Pearl Street; Stone Street was called Spring Street; Springside Avenue was called Rock Street; Fitch Street was called East Street; Crescent Street was called Beaver Street or Pond Street; and Pine Rock Avenue was called North Street.

CHURCHES OF NEW HAVEN: WESTVILLE CONGREGATIONAL

New Haven Register, February 2, 1930
By Elsie Roberts

Hard against historic West Rock stands the Westville Congregational Church, the dark mass of the mountain forming an excellent background for an edifice that has sheltered an unbroken succession of worshippers for nearly a century.

The early history of this church is lost in the dim past, but it is well known that until the year 1832 there was no Congregational church in the town of Westville, although there was a strong settlement of churchgoing people on that side of the West River. They followed the rural custom of driving into town to church, going probably to Center Church on the Green.

In 1832, an ecclesiastical society having been formed, services were held in the conference room of the village schoolhouse, which was also used as a place of worship by the newly organized Methodist society of Westville.

Four years passed before the little band was to build a house of worship but by 1838 the present building was erected and dedicated.

The first pastor was the Reverend Judson Root, principal of the boys' school in the village. After his demise, the church was served for a number of years by itinerant clergymen who divided their time between Westville and other parishes.

A drive for a Sunday school was launched and in 1922 the present roomy parish house was dedicated and opened for use. Its Colonial lines harmonize admirably with the ancient edifice of which it is a part and built, as it is, in the rear of the church building, it is convenient to the house of worship and yet not close enough to detract from the simple beauty of the edifice with its plain lines and graceful white spire.

A large gymnasium in the parish house provides recreational opportunities for young people and volleyball, basketball and other sports are offered under the leadership of competent directors. The Boy Scouts and Camp Fire Girls hold their meetings there and under the able direction of Frank Nicholas, superintendent, the Sunday school is a thriving institution.

Westville Methodist Church Marks Its Fiftieth Anniversary Sunday

New Haven Evening Register, November 8, 1944

Beginning in Westville in 1810, when the Reverend Olive Sykes preached in the community, Methodism did not attract many converts until 1815, when a class of five women was organized. Miss Harriett Hitchcock was the first Methodist in Westville.

Building Committee
After meeting for years in an old school building, a building committee in 1850 composed of Augustus Parker, Guy C. Hotchkiss and Lucius W.

In part of a stereoscopic view from around 1875, two prominent, long-vanished buildings stand in front of West Rock ridge. The building on the left-hand side was the Westville School, built in 1870 and designed by New Haven architect David R. Brown. The school was replaced by the present synagogue, built in 1971. The building on the right-hand side was Westville Methodist Church, built in 1852, and later destroyed by fire on February 19, 1893. *Photographed by Henry S. Peck. Courtesy of Joseph Taylor.*

Peck planned for a church building. Dedicated on August 4, 1852, the new building was used until 1893, when it burned to the ground.

Meanwhile, services were held in the Masonic Hall on Whalley Avenue. On Sunday, June 17, 1894, the present building was dedicated.

WESTVILLE ME CHURCH, PRETTY VILLAGE EDIFICE BURNED TO BLACK AND GRAY ASHES

New Haven Daily Palladium, February 20, 1893
Little Ribbon of Flaunting Flame Seen Too Late at the Gable Peak—Church Just Free From Debt—Loss and Insurance—Where Services Will Now Be Held.

The Westville ME Church in an hour yesterday morning was reduced to a heap of black and gray ashes. The building was a wooden structure with gable roof and cathedral glass windows. It was valued at $15,000 and had just been cleared of all debt. There was an insurance of only $6,000 on it.

At 9:15 a.m. a thin flaunting ribbon of flame was seen at the peak of the roof. An alarm was forthwith sounded and the Westville fire company under Captain Murdock Dingwall responded. Other villagers assisted with buckets of water. It caught from the furnace that had been heated for service at 10:30 a.m., and spread through the rib timbers of the walls.

FLAME SEEN TOO LATE

The fire had been burning unseen throughout the lining of one side of the church, and when that little ribbon of flame was seen flaunting at the gable peak, the blaze was beyond all prospect of control. But the firemen and the villagers worked with grim zeal. The New Haven companies did not go to the scene, it is beyond the city limits, and before the New Haven firemen could get there the building would have been all burned. The pastor, the Reverend William McNichol, Superintendent William H. Farnham of the Sunday school and Trustees John N. Austin, A.N. Farnham, W.E. Woodmansee, G.E. Millar, J.S. Dickerman, C. Smith and W.W. Fox are all very sad over the sudden catastrophe. The church was built in 1851 and lately received some elaborate interior repairs. It was in a thrifty condition and the members were congratulating themselves on its final absolute freedom from debt. While the fire was raging, A.L. Scripture was keeping the crowd out of range of the likely fall of the chimney. He was leaning against a fence when the chimney did fall.

STRUCK WITH HOT BRICKS

The topmost bricks struck him full in the face and knocked him through the fence. The bricks were hot and his cheeks and nose were burned. He escaped, though, with no serious injury. No one else suffered any mishap. Opposite the church stands the brick outhouse. The roof of this was scorched by the intense heat and water had to be piled on it to save the building from catching ablaze.

The only fortunate fact about the church fire is that it did not break out when the congregation was at service. When the time for service came, on the site of the pretty village church stood a smoking, smoldering mound of ashes and melted, twisted brass and glass.

Whether the congregation will forthwith begin to rebuild has not yet been decided. The church members are deeply discouraged but they will likely decide to erect another church soon. Meanwhile services will be held in one of the halls of the village. There were no services yesterday, as everything was all confusion and gloom.

WESTVILLE METHODISTS HAVE CAUSE FOR JOY

New Haven Daily Palladium, June 18, 1894
It Replaces the One Burned Last Year—Large Congregations At All the Exercises—Bishop Foss Conducts the Ceremonies—Large Fund Subscribed

A fire on the morning of February 19, 1893, destroyed the Westville ME Church. Since that time the little band of 114 members and a congregation of about twice that number have put forth efforts to rebuild. They have been rewarded, for yesterday Bishop Foss dedicated to the worship of God the handsome church of which the Westville Methodists may be justly proud.

The new building is of red sandstone and wood, one story, Gothic, with a small tower. Inside it is one of the prettiest churches in the city.

There are six memorial windows, one of which is to the memory of the Reverend Arthur MacMicholl, former pastor, and a brother of the Reverend W. McNichol, the present pastor.

The congregation of the Westville Methodist Church built this building in 1894 after its older church burned down the year prior on February 19, 1893. This circa 1907 postcard view shows that building with three young girls in front. This church also burned down on April 13, 1971. *Courtesy of Joseph Taylor.*

The structure cost $13,800, of which $11,800 had already been pledged yesterday morning and most if it has been paid. The organ was built by George Jardine, of New York, at a cost of $1,500.

CHURCHES OF NEW HAVEN: ST. JAMES

New Haven Register, December 15, 1929

A meeting of the inhabitants of Westville to consider the formation of an Episcopal Society was held on January 13, 1835. The title of "Union Episcopal Church of St. James Parish" was adopted but was changed at an annual meeting of the parish in 1836, to "St. James Parish."

The matter of erecting a building being of first importance, the members of the parish devoted themselves to raising funds. Meanwhile, services were held in Pendleton's Inn in Westville. Stanton Pendleton, who owned the inn, was himself an ardent Episcopalian and a vestryman of St. James Parish.

Acting for the parish, Mr. Pendleton bought eight acres of land near Edgewood Park and laid it out in forty-eight building lots with two streets. Through the exertions of Mr. Pendleton and the Reverend Stephen Jewett, the lots were sold for $75 apiece, the total sales amounting to $3,600. The profit to the parish was $2,730.

A lot on Whalley Avenue was purchased and the building of the church begun. The cornerstone was laid June 21, 1837, construction was completed in May 1839 and the new edifice opened for worship on June 10 of the same year. A rectory was built in 1853 and was occupied first by Reverend Henry McGlory, rector from 1852 to 1855.

The residents of Westville, "substantial business men with interests in the city of New Haven and affiliations with local industries—a paper mill and a match factory," welcomed the new church with genuine cordiality and the enthusiasm of a devoted congregation carried it through the trials and difficulties incident to the formation of a new parish.

In 1919, seventy-three years after its completion, the church building showed decided signs of age, and the only remedy was to rebuild.

Accordingly, on December 11, 1916, the rector, J. Frederick Sexton, called a meeting of some of the most interested parishioners to consider the organization of a corporation, without capital stock, to raise funds for the purpose of acquiring real estate and erecting a building.

This postcard view of Saint James Episcopal Church from around 1910 shows its brick edifice where it was once located on the north side of Whalley Avenue between Harrison and Emerson Streets. The church was built in 1837 and its first officiator was Reverend Alonzo B. Chapin. *Photographed by the Beck Manufacturing Co. Courtesy of Colin M. Caplan.*

This was done, a plot of ground on the corner of Marvel Road and West Elm Street was bought and a handsome new parish house erected and dedicated April 1, 1923. Later, a new rectory was built and the old one, together with the first church on Whalley Avenue, put on sale. The proceeds will be used to swell the funds for other new buildings.

At the present time services are being held in the parish house, but as soon as the standing indebtedness is cleared away a handsome new church will be erected opposite the parish house.

WESTVILLE CEMETERY

By Florence Woodmansee, 1923

Upon the petition of a committee representing the inhabitants of the Westfield District, the General Assembly of Connecticut, which met in New Haven the first Wednesday in May 1832, resolved that a society should be constituted by the name of the School Society of Westfield, possessed all the powers and privileges of other school societies and that all bills and obligations either of or to the old society be transferred to the new one.

At the first meeting, duly warned for and held upon June 7, 1832, it was resolved that the new society should be known as the Westville School District and there begins the calling of this section by the name it was thereafter to be known.

Dating from this early meeting, for a period extending over well nigh ninety years, members of this school board and their successors, supplemented by the efforts of a Village Improvement Society, founded in 1848, forerunner of the Edgewood Civic Association that was instituted in 1908, exercised a patriarchal oversight upon matters of import pertaining to civic economics and community welfare, including that of the cemetery.

On February 6, 1833, Michael G. Hotchkiss transferred to the Westville School District 1 acre, 3 rods and 2/10 of a rod.

This, undoubtedly, was the original "God Acre" of the Westville Cemetery.

At the crest of the hill upon the cityward side of the river (near to the historic spot above the old ford, where that gallant, little band of local militiamen had made their heroic stand against the invading British troops in 1779), the situation for the purpose selected was an admirable one.

True, the soil was sandy, savin, locust and scraggling wild cherry growth abounding, but the tract was level and easily adaptable to the regulation layout of cemetery aisles and lots.

In 1834, a committee was appointed upon the matter of a fence and also to take up the matter of clearing the scrub from the land, etc. In the early forties a hearse was purchased and housed within the cemetery bounds, said hearse being furnished (at a suitable rate) to surrounding towns, when not in use within the Westville District.

Another half century elapsed and the cemetery was no longer a thinly populated city of the dead, but a crowded acre of lots, all now in possession of individual ownership, most of the plots occupied at least in part, some to capacity, and the old School Society no longer had jurisdiction.

And now arose the need of an accession of land and a small tract to the north of the original plot, on the slope toward Blake Street side, was purchased as the personal enterprises of the late Wilfred Ford, then sexton; the land was terraced and offered for sale, either in plots or for individual graves.

On September 26, 1885, John M. Lines of Woodbridge, Connecticut, who owned the tract adjoining the original cemetery plot, easterly extending well beyond its bounds, from Whalley Avenue northerly to Blake Street, quit claimed said tract, comprising some three acres, more or less, to a new association, formed solely as a business proposition for the disposal of the land for burial purposes, said association being duly incorporated and known as the Westville Cemetery Association, Inc. West of this tract of land, below the terraces northwest of the original plot, lies the "Potters Field," its rank upon rank of humble graves mutely testifying to the fact that the old act of the early thirties, ordering the bodies of the unclaimed pauper dead should be turned over to Medical Associations for dissection, met with a most determined opposition in New Haven and when the "corner for the poor" in the original plot was no longer available, the town provided a suitable strip for such interments here.

Opposite the north end of Edgewood Park, on Whalley Avenue, are the two cemeteries—Mishkan Israel, or Jewish, and Westville. Mishkan Israel has a substantial and attractive iron fence and is a credit to the neighborhood. Westville has both hedge and a wooden fence, neither of which are in good repair or tidy condition. Division fence and dividing lines between these cemeteries have been removed and cordial good will exists among the lot owners and managers of both.

Mishkan Israel Cemetery was founded in 1843 as the state's first Jewish cemetery. In 1910, the brownstone mortuary chapel was built there, designed by Westville resident Ferdinand Von Beren.

WESTVILLE FIRE STATION

New Haven Register, March 14, 1915

Another attractive building that is soon to be erected in Westville is the engine house. Bids are now being received for the new house, which is to be erected at the corner of Fountain and Harrison Streets. The architects for the building are Brown & Von Beren. The new building will be very much in keeping with the residences in that locality.

The style of architecture is the American Colonial of the Georgian period. The exterior falls are to be of North Haven selected pallet brick laid with a Dutch bond with raked out joints. The roof of variegated green and purple slate, with a cupola containing a bell. The first story is arranged for a large apparatus room, police station and workroom, with toilet room connecting. The second floor is arranged for a large assembly room, three bedrooms, one committee room and toilet room with shower. In the cellar is arranged a hose drying rack; a fireproof vault for storage of records, also coal bins, tank room, etc.

The first floor is of fireproof construction with a cement finished floor. The ceiling is of metal. The inside trim is of No. 1 North Carolina pine, stained. The building is heated by a direct steam gravity system.

Westville has been sadly in need of a new fire engine house for a long time. The present building is a small wooden affair without a cellar and is wholly unfit for all its uses in cold weather; for that matter, since the fire auto has been added, the quarters were entirely too small.

The company is a volunteer one and was organized July 28, 1890, by Amos Dickerman. The first meeting was held at the home of the late W.H. Cheney on Barnett Street.

The officers elected were George W. Hemman, foreman; Murdock Dingwall, assistant foreman; L.H. Cheney, secretary; Carlyle Mansfield, treasurer. The fire commissioners were Amos Dickerman, who has taken an active interest in the company from its inception until the present day; also William S. Beecher and Burton Dickerman. The members were Edward Baldwin, George Hinman, James Sinclair, Carlyle Mansfield, Patrick Murray, Thomas Gold, L.G. Hemingway, R.C. McClure, Ernest Doolittle, L.H. Cheney, John McGuire, George Hopkins, Charles Bradley, Henry Daniels, Frank Munn, Henry Van Housen, A. Perkins, W.W. Sperry, James Mercer, Henry Goodman, Frank Pitcher Van Bartholomew, Frederick Reynolds, M. Welch, Alexander Fraser, Alvin Hull, Theodore Shumway, Murdock Dingwall and Dan Bremner. The last four named are still active members of the company. Dan Bremner is assistant engineer and "Cap" Shumway, as he is affectionately called, seldom misses a fire and is just as active as any member of the present company.

M. Dingwall was chief of the department for twenty years. The second meeting was in C.H. Mansfield's market on Whalley Avenue.

The original name of the company was the Dickerman Hose Company. The jumper that was used by the fire ladies in those days was purchased in July 1890 and was kept in Joseph Payne's barn until the dedication of the present house on November 10, 1890. The first meeting in their new quarters was on December 10 of the same year.

The hook and ladder went into service November 7, 1898, and on December 13 of that year the name was changed to the Westville Hook and Ladder Company. On November 10 a hose wagon was added to the company's equipments, and on September 20, 1910, the auto truck came into use. Westville set the example in this vicinity; it had the first fire auto in the city.

When the auto was purchased, it was decided by the district to have an engineer who would stay permanently at the firehouse. David B. Mercer was appointed by the school board to fill this position; later an associate was appointed to help him. One man takes a week at night duty and the other a week of day duty in alternation.

When the company was originally organized it obtained its house and lot and full equipment by subscriptions and affairs given for that purpose. In November 1913, the school district purchased the apparatus and furnishings of the house. The house and lot still belong to the company.

The officers and members of the present company are Chief David B. Mercer; Captain A.J. Graff; First Lieutenant C.H. Meade; Second Lieutenant Alexander Dingwall; secretary Wilbur Smith; treasurer W.D. Payne; chaplain Reverend J. Frederick Sexton; department physician Dr. O.W. Marsh; company physician Dr. W.N. Winne; trustees C.H. Meade and A.J. Graff; and fire commissioners Amos Dickerman, M.J. Powers, George M. Griswold, P.R. Greist and J.B. Tower.

The members are Dan Bremner, Theodore Shumway, A.S. Hull, Curtiss Ford, Murdock Dingwall, Harold E. Smith, J.J. Shepperd, Roy Taylor, W.S. Baldwin, Jack Atkins, Dennis Ahearn, T.G. Burton, C.E. Cordery, William C. Clingan, T. Delaurius, W. Moer, Kenneth Howland, James W. Jolly, S. Knous, George Kiley, Emil Kluth, Robert N. Lattin, William D. Mercer, James Oris, Gus Roth, William Ruschenberg, A.J. Smith, Tom Wilson, J. Walsh, Paul Wittlesey, Howard Graff, Carl Widman and David E. Alling. There are twenty-four honorary members, one of whom is Chief Rufus Fancher.

The firemen have fought some big fires since they were organized, and it can be said that they have worked to the best of their ability. Their work compares favorably with any organized company in this city.

Their first big fire was at one o'clock on the night their house was dedicated. The firemen had had a big parade and a celebration in connection with the dedication. They had just retired to their homes when they were called to fight a fire in the Lounsberry slaughterhouse on Whalley Avenue, next to the Episcopal church. This was followed soon after by the Cheney shop on Whalley Avenue. On three different occasions they were called out to fight big fires at the Diamond Match Factory, now occupied by the Geometric Tool Company. Another big blaze was the Sperry Hall on Whalley Avenue, near West River bridge. They were called to save the Yale grandstand, and at another time the bleachers. Miller's grocery store and the livery stables on Whalley Avenue were hard fires to fight. The Westville house was still another hard-fought battle.

The Pond Lily Paper Mill made a big conflagration when it burned nearly twenty years ago. Perhaps the worst fire the company ever had to battle was the Methodist church, which was burned to the ground over twenty years ago. J.P. Hauser's wagon shop was a most spectacular blaze and was seen for miles around. All these fires and others perhaps equally as large happened before the automobile was a part of the company's equipment.

On July 25, 1911, at 7:30 a.m. the Lake Burton icehouse started to burn. The auto worked 16½ hours at this fire. For the first 7 hours the engine ran without a stop, lifting water from the lake. This was another spectacular blaze; this house had burned twice before. On January 6, 1912, at 10:30 a.m.—an extremely cold day, five above zero—Mrs. E.W. Cooper's home on Whalley Avenue burned. The firemen kept the blaze from spreading to nearby dwellings despite the fact that the water froze as soon as it touched the house.

The burning of the Elm City icehouses on January 18, 1912, started at 1:50 a.m. and kept breaking out anew in the sawdust after it was apparently all extinguished. The men were called to the scene of the fire seven times, working altogether about eighty hours.

A.N. Farnham's barn on May 6, 1913, at 4:00 a.m. was another big blaze. The men worked about five hours pumping water from the stream nearby. On previous occasions the Westville firemen have been called to fires at A.N. Farnham's.

The Konold icehouse burning about a year ago adds another fire to the list of big conflagrations in Westville.

When the Westville School District was established in 1833, it created three school districts: middle, east and west. The Middle District schoolhouse was called Franklin Hall and was originally located on what is now Harrison Street. Around 1870, it was moved to the bottom of Fountain Street and again moved in the 1880s to Whalley Avenue, where it was attached to an old house and became part of the Edgewood Hotel. It still exists at the corner of Central and Whalley Avenues, although its appearance was altered in 1913. The East District schoolhouse was located at the corner of Fitch and Blake Streets. It was moved to 27 Willard Street and converted into a house

The old firehouse was here at Alden Avenue and Fountain Street, built in 1890 when the department was called the Dickerman Hose Company. In 1893, it changed its name to the Westville Fire Department and on September 20, 1910, it was the first fire company in New Haven to purchase an auto truck. This postcard view was taken shortly after the purchase of this Seagrave fire engine. *Courtesy of Colin M. Caplan.*

in 1872. The West District schoolhouse was built at the corner of Fountain Street and Marvel Road and is now a residence. The schools were consolidated into a new schoolhouse in 1870.

BENTON SCHOOL NAMED FOR TEACHER

New Haven Register, December 12, 1928

The Mary Frances Benton School, situated on Whalley Avenue at the corner of Harrison Street, was built in 1870 and was at the time under the jurisdiction of the Westville school system. It was for many years called the Westville School and not until 1915 was it named in honor of Miss Benton.

Miss Benton was born June 23, 1833, and taught in the schools here from 1867 until 1900. She was one of the most beloved teachers of this city and in 1915, two years after her death, a number of the men and women of Westville who had gone to school with her named the Westville School in her honor. On June 24 of that year they placed a bronze tablet on the school with memorial ceremonies.

The tablet reads:

> Frances Benton Memorial School Dedicated June 24, 1915
> To enduringly record the virtues of a noble woman this bronze is placed
> as love's tribute from her "Boys and Girls."
> For 33 successive years she taught in the Westville District.
> She loved always and was always loved
> Mary Frances Benton
> 1867 Teacher 1900
> Born June 23, 1833. Died May 12, 1913

In 1920 the Westville schools were taken over by the Board of Education of New Haven. Lillian D. Knowlton is principal of the school.

Sheriden School Named for Teacher

New Haven Register, May 12, 1929

The Susan S. Sheridan Junior High School on Fountain Street was built in 1924 and named for Dr. Susan S. Sheridan, for fifty years a teacher in the New Haven public schools and one of the most beloved instructors in the city schools. During her half a century of work she did much toward the organization and perfection of the English Department in the high school and also organized a number of literary clubs, most of which are named for her.

Susan S. Sheridan was born October 33, 1852, and was the daughter of Patrick and Susan Smith Sheridan. At the time of her death in July 1928, she was the last surviving member of her family, her three sisters and parents having died some time before. Dr. Sheridan started her career as a teacher in 1871, one year after her graduation from high school. She later studied at the University of Omaha and in 1897 received the degree of BA. In 1902 she received her PhD from Yale University.

She specialized in English, organized the Department of English and was the head of it at the time of her death. She also helped organize the lecture courses at Albertus Magnus College and was in charge of the Sunday meetings of the Catholic Social Service Society.

The students of Sheridan Junior High School posed for this photo in 1943. The school was built in 1924 and designed by Westville resident Ferdinand Von Beren's architectural firm, Brown & Von Beren. *Courtesy of Colin M. Caplan.*

The school named in honor of her is one of the most modern buildings in the city. It is of brick construction and contains twenty-five rooms. The lot, building, furniture and equipment cost approximately $238,355. Arthur C. Klock is principal at the present time.

DONALD G. MITCHELL MEMORIAL LIBRARY

New Haven Union, December 1, 1912

The library is quartered in the room used by the late Ebenezer B. Beecher as his private art gallery and it makes an ideal reading room because it is so well lighted and so handsomely finished. About 2,500 volumes have been loaned by the New Haven Public Library directors and the association owns about 2,500 more. There is an average circulation of some 2,000 volumes per month, which is a very encouraging fact. It is hoped that the number of books available will be greatly increased, as the demand is showing a steady gain. Besides the books, there are several interesting relics and souvenirs in the building. One of Dr. Marvel's desks is to be seen there and many of his first copies are now the property of the association.

It has been stated that as soon as the members can provide a suitable room and suitable means for caring for the possessions, many of the rare books, much of this manuscript and some historical things of interest in connection with the life of Mr. Mitchell will be placed in charge of the organization by the relatives of the late author.

The Beecher Memorial Park is a splendid plot of two acres in the heart of the settlement and it is a fitting location for the library, too. Many people enjoy the park and in the summertime many sit there to read. It also affords a breathing space for the people, which will be of increasing value as the open spaces are closed up by the rapid strides made in building up the section.

This property was the home of the late Ebenezer B. Beecher of Westville, who was the founder of the famous Diamond Match Company.

The plan to establish the library and reading room in memory of the late Donald G. Mitchell met with instant favor, and though the subscriptions were not started until the last days of July 1919, about $10,000 was subscribed up to January 1, 1911, for the purpose. This amount enabled the temporary committee to secure for a library site for the Beecher property.

The Donald Grant Mitchell Memorial Library was an estate called Blondale and was sold to Westville in 1910 after the death of its former occupant, industrialist Ebenezer B. Beecher. This circa 1910 postcard view shows the extensive mansion, which was originally a much smaller house built by a mason named Theodore Hotchkiss in the early nineteenth century. The building was replaced by the present library in 1965. *Courtesy of Joseph Taylor.*

Some form of organization was necessary to legally hold and manage the property and a corporation without capital stock was formed under the laws of Connecticut, bearing the name of the Donald G. Mitchell Library and Beecher Park Memorial, Inc., and officers were elected November 1, 1910.

The Beecher property was purchased at $16,000,000, a cash payment being made of $8,000 and a mortgage being given for the remainder. The deeds were passed November 21, 1910. The price was a low one considering the size and location of the property, which is by far the best now available in Westville for public purposes. The grounds, which are of about two acres in extent, centrally located and attractively planted with trees and shrubs, will be called Beecher Park in memory of the Beecher family.

Mr. Herbert F. Larkin is the librarian of the association. The officers are W.E. Britton, president; L. Wheeler Beecher, vice-president; Howard E. Adt, secretary treasurer; Walter L. Mitchell, George Dudley Seymour, P. Raymond Greist, Reverend J.F. Sexton, Reverend J.J. McGiveny, George W. Crane, John R. Tower, William C. Harmon, Charles E. Brown, Walter T. Hart, Reverend C.F. Luther and Charles T. Lincoln.

The advisory board consists of Arthur T. Hadley, Anson Phelps Stokes, Thomas R. Lounsbury, William Lyon Phelps, Norris G. Osborn, Louis C. Tiffany, Charles Scribner and Arthur Reed Kimball.

SECRET PANEL FOUND IN WESTVILLE LIBRARY

New Haven Register, September 20, 1936
By Gladys Solomon
WPA Worker's Discovery Recalls Life of Ebenezer Beecher, New Haven Inventor and Match King, Who Once Lived Where Public Library Stands

A match that still lights fires around the world was first struck in Westville's Public Library! And—according to hearsay—the ghost of the man who struck it still wanders through the rooms of his old mansion or sits on the dog-shaped stone that guards the building!

When the clock strikes twelve, midnight, and the stacks of books are cloaked in darkness, old Ebenezer Beecher, inventor of the wooden match machine, glides down the stairs to his study and fumbles behind the secret panels to see if his patents are safe. Sometimes he pauses, in his descent, to pull out the drawer cunningly fitted into the bottom step and rearrange the valuables hidden therein. The drawer is there—empty now, to be sure—but what better testimony could one ask of the inventive genius and character of the man?

To anyone unacquainted with the history of the place, the Donald G. Mitchell Library in Beecher Park, Westville, looks like nothing but a charming gray stucco English country house with trimmings of dark timber. Although the entrance is at 37 Harrison Street, the north side faces West Rock. An unusually attractive public building, surrounded by spacious lawns and towering trees, it is noticed by everyone who drives through Westville by way of Whalley Avenue.

ANOTHER HOUSE

Beneath its stucco surface, however, are the walls of another house—an old Colonial mansion formerly belonging to Ebenezer Beecher. This house was sold to the town of Westville in 1910 to settle his estate, and transformed into a library named in honor of Donald G. Mitchell, famous literary man of Forest Road. A late contemporary of Washington Irving, he wrote many widely read books, his best known being *Dream Life* and *Reveries of a Bachelor*. Mitchell's pen name, "Ik Marvel," is perhaps more familiar than his own.

After the library had been in operation for ten years or so, the building was completely remodeled—both inside and out—and brought to its present appearance. But the general plan of the old structure may still be discerned and the trapdoor that Ebenezer had built into the floor of his dining room may still be observed in the ceiling of the cellar.

Recently, WPA workers redecorating the interior of the house came upon the secret drawer in the bottom step of the second-floor staircase. It had been covered with a carpet, but when this was removed so that the stairs could be painted, the worker assigned to the job noticed a small handle just below the step. He pulled. Out came a drawer exactly the shape of a hollow step. But, although reports have spread through Westville that it was filled with jewels and banknotes, the truth of the matter is that it was empty.

Then Sherman Wesley, at work on the American Guide for the Writers' Project, began making inquiries about who had built it. Miss Lambert, the librarian, remembered a secret panel behind a bookcase in the northwest sidewall. She had known about it for a long time. Indeed, Mr. Herbert F. Larkin, the original librarian, had found drawings of Beecher's match machine concealed there. These drawings are at present being preserved in the library's vault.

Secret Passageway

One thing led to another, and soon an old resident of the town remembered that there was a secret passageway leading to a private retreat in the basement. A new floor had been laid since Ebenezer's time, so the trapdoor could not be found upstairs, but a careful examination of the ceiling in the cellar actually revealed the outlines of a door.

When the children who come to the library heard about the secret panels, stairs and trapdoors, they let their imaginations run wild. Soon stories began to circulate to the effect that Mitchell Library was haunted, and every night the white-bearded inventor came out of the closet of a second-story room—the chamber in which he died—and prowled about the place. No one to date has admitted seeing the ghost, but—in the minds of the children at least—he is there.

The Beechers were one of the most prominent families in Westville. There were four brothers in it—Ebenezer, William, Lyman and Wheeler. They lived on the corner of what is now Fountain and Harrison Streets, although at the time Harrison Street was known as Franklin Street. All of them became well known in civic and industrial circles.

Invented Match Machine

Ebenezer was the inventor. He was born in Morris, Connecticut, in 1874, and as a child was quiet and studious, puttering around with tools and machinery and forever making drawings of wheels and levers. When he was still a young man, he perfected his invention of a machine to make combustible wooden matches. He and his brother built a factory at the base of West Rock—where the Geometric Tool Company is now located—and began the manufacture of matches. Later they formed a company that at first was called the Swift, Courtney & Beecher Match Company, and then became known by its trademark as the Diamond Match Company.

Ebenezer made a fortune on his invention. He built a large two-story Colonial house on the family property. He had the rounds developed into gardens and a fountain played gracefully on the lawn. He had arbors erected and paths laid out. He became the typical country gentleman, with a coach and four, a gardener and a bevy of servants. And as his money came in, he added to the house, until it contained twenty-five rooms.

Unique Stone

The large stones that may still be seen around the estate are a story in themselves. Most interesting of the lot is the "sculptured" stone, worn by erosion in a stream to the shape of a small dog. It now stands on a slate slab facing Whalley Avenue.

These stones are not native rocks. Although Ebenezer had a whole mountain at his door, he preferred the stones of Morris, Connecticut, his birthplace, to Westville's traprock. In particular, he longed to have for his garden a "dog stone" that lay in the center of a brook near his old home and on which he used to sit and dream as a boy. So one day the order went forth to Morris to send the "dog" and half a dozen other rocks out to Westville. Four yolk of oxen were required to haul the load, and you can imagine the amazement of the neighbors when the curious cargo arrived.

But Ebenezer was happy. He had his boyhood souvenir, and he used to sit at the bay window in his study and gaze at it for hours.

Fortune Slips Away

As the inventor grew older, his fortune began to dwindle. Patents were stolen, investments proved worthless and frequent loans to struggling investors ate it away. Knowing Ebenezer Beecher's generosity and trusting nature, many poor machine designers and some out-and-out grafters imposed upon the man until in desperation he refused to open his door to anyone but old friends.

He would sit at the bay window brooding over the past, and when he noticed a stranger coming up the walk, he'd lock the door and climb hastily down into his secret retreat in the cellar. There he would stay and work over machine designs until he was sure the caller had gone.

On the second floor of his home, Ebenezer had a large room called the gallery. In it were dozens of watercolor and oil paintings in heavy gilt frames. The collection, which was considered very valuable, was sold at his death in 1904.

"Blondale," as Ebenezer called his estate, is now Beecher Park and a public domain. But the old coach house still stands behind the library, as does the ivy-covered brick laundry building. This brick building has become known—for no good reason—as the "slave house," although no slaves ever lived there. At one time, however, it was used by the Westville Fire Department.

On Harrison Street next door to the library is a pleasant two-story home owned by Mrs. Helena Hemingway, Ebenezer's only daughter. Mrs. Hemingway, a gracious, gray-haired lady, received your reporter in a drawing room hung with paintings from the old Beecher gallery. She lived near her father until he died at the age of seventy-four, and, as far as she could observe, he never once hid in the cellar, although he did shun strangers because he had lost so much money in loans that were never repaid.

When I told her the legend and traditions that have grown up about his mansion, she threw back her head and laughed wholeheartedly.

"Ghosts!" she exclaimed. "That's too good, really!"

The old library was remodeled in 1921, designed by Westville resident Frederick Von Beren. The building was torn down and replaced in 1965.

MODERN MERLINS RIGHT HERE IN OUR MIDST

New Haven Register, September 12, 1926
Magicians Powell and Petrie Outdo Mystics of Far East in Accomplishments—Both Keen Students of Science Since Boyhood—Recognized as Experts

Dwarfed beneath the towering, stony prominence of West Rock, and situated in a little garden spot in Valley Road, Westville, where the setting sun casts its deepest shadows, stands a neat white house, the joint home of two men whose fame is worldwide.

A wide trail, trod alike by the mightiest and lowliest, is beaten to the door of the house as well as to the two-story frame workshop nearby—but more of that later on.

These two men are Frederick Eugene Powell, dean of the Society of American Magicians and vice-president of the International Society of Magicians; and John. A. Petrie, president of the Lewis-Petrie Company, manufacturers of nine-tenths of the illusions used by modern-day magicians.

Two no greater men in the art of legerdemain are living today. There are no two men engaged in the practice of that art whose names are accorded more ringing acclaim.

Has Air of Teacher

A brief description of the two. Dean Powell is a teacher. His dignified appearance, courteous address and demeanor in general all thoroughly impress it upon you. He is recognized as such by his fellow craftsmen who have bestowed upon him the title of "Dean."

The square set of his shoulders, the clear, sparkling black eyes, the ruddy complexion; all belie the seventy-one years to which he admits. The youthfulness that cloaks him makes you forget the thinning thatch of white hair and white moustaches.

To describe his confrere, John Petrie, is to describe a man grown from a youth with a determination to succeed. Both men are, as a matter of fact, the products of successfully carrying out youthful ambitions, the quality being intensely desirous of achieving a certain goal. Those ambitions acquired when these two sages of magic were young have been and still are carefully nurtured years after their success was assured.

Petrie a Thinker

John Petrie is a tall, angular man with the hands and face of a genius—a dreamer whose dreams spring into material being. His eyes are those of a thinker—they are calculating eyes—eyes behind which there is a brain that has conceived 90 percent of the apparati used by conjurers these many years.

Like Dean Powell, there is something of the air of a teacher about him, but it is surcharged with a quick, nervous energy that characterizes the man who spends his time solving the secrets of science.

He is a Yankee—Connecticut Yankee, who has given the mysterious Chinese a new magic; who has penetrated the secrets of the black arts of

India and the entire Orient and given to the practitioners new and better methods. Truly his name is a watchword throughout the world.

"The sun never sets on his clients," Dean Powell said.

John Petrie, it is amazing to know, is the inventor of the modern-day gasoline engine magneto. A desire to do away with the cumbersome set of batteries carried in early machines gave birth to the idea from which grew the magneto of today. Modern automobile hardware grew out of designs by Mr. Petrie.

John Petrie, as he appeared to this reporter, might have stepped from a Ben Ames Williams novel.

Leaders in Field

John Petrie manufactures magical apparatus. Those who have trod the path to buy to his door include Houdini, Manuel and scores of others including Herrmann. Those who have trod the same path to hear the words of wisdom from Dean Powell have included the same luminaries in the world of now you see it and now you don't.

Here is an amazing thing, a complete refutation of a popular fallacy.

"The quickness of the hand does not deceive the eye."

That, if you please, is a statement of fact from no less authority than Dean Powell. And to prove it he slowly vanished this reporter's last half dollar to the complete mystification of its owner and the camera wrecker who has pictorial proof of the ease (?) with which things vanish.

"It is the mis en scene—the atmosphere which the magician creates rather than any rapid motion with the hands which fools the eyes," was the manner in which he argued his surprising statement.

What really started Dean Powell on the road to his present position of the "greatest of all living illusionists" was his glimpse at the mysteries of Senor Fritz, which in 1853 held forth at Ninth and Chestnut Streets, Philadelphia.

"I was but seven years old at the time, but what I saw made a deep impression," he reminisced. "I was twelve years old when I saw the great Robert Hellar and that settled it."

A natural ability for analysis and mathematics aided the budding magician tremendously and by the age of sixteen he had given his first public performance. The boy, who was to one day become the accepted guest in the best homes of our country because of his uncanny ability in the creation of illusions, had arrived, and only four years later he made his first public appearance.

"I lived in Chester, Pennsylvania, and I went to Pittsburgh to give the performance," Dean Powell said. "I was twenty years old but I never was so lonesome and homesick in all my life. But after that first week I lost that feeling."

Fifty-four years of being before the public followed.

Dean Powell interrupted to say that he had been a student at the Pennsylvania Military Academy, and after his graduation was called to serve as an instructor in mathematics. This post he held three years before becoming a professional exponent of the art of legerdemain.

Placing the coin in his right hand (apparently) he closed his fingers about it and when he opened them the coin was gone. Then came the majestic pass and the left hand was opened to show that it was not there. Then without a single bit of the usual "presto chango" stuff the coin was found to have been in the right hand all the time, much to this writer's relief and his lens hound's amazement.

Of course there might have been a certain lack of mental agility on the part of this spy, but Dean Powell was less than three feet away when he performed the feat. Every motion was careful, precise, calculated—had no "quickness-of-the-hand-will-deceive-the-eye" stuff about it at all.

The same technique was employed in vanishing the silk handkerchief—a trick that is illustrated elsewhere on this page. It was done slowly in order to allow the photographer to catch the various poses. But the illusion was just the same as in the coin trick.

These two tricks are elemental, it was explained. They were displayed to this writer merely to illustrate a certain point—the point being that the quickness of the hand does not deceive the eye.

The house that Mr. Powell and Mr. Petrie lived in was an old colonial-era house once located at 152 Valley Street. The building burned down in the 1970s and is now the site of another house.

BUILDERS OF BOWL A LOCAL COMPANY

New Haven Journal-Courier, November 21, 1914

The Sperry Engineering Company of this city builders of the Yale Bowl in a concern organized for general engineering, designing and structural work.

The Bowl, while not by any means the largest or most expensive work accomplished by the company, is perhaps the more noticeable than any other work of theirs, attracting attention from Maine to Frisco.

The Bowl if placed diagonally on the green would overlap the five streets, College, Temple, Church, Elm and Chapel.

Although some persons claimed that the Bowl would not be handled by a local firm, this concern has not only carried out its work successfully but has completed it on time, also handling ten other contracts not originally in the specifications.

One of the most interesting of its enterprises at present in hand is the stadium at the new Yale athletic grounds. Although the work is scarcely out of the preliminary stages, the structure, owing to its novel plan and huge seating prospects, is the subject of a popular interest that is likely to increase until the structure is completed and stands out as the greatest thing of its kind in all the world.

The Bowl is oval in plan and presents a beautiful view in the symmetry and simplicity of its design. It will cover an area of twelve and a half acres

The largest structure in New Haven is the Yale Bowl, constructed in 1914 in the center of a large block near the West Haven line. The Bowl was the largest arena built in the world and was designed by engineer Charles A. Ferry. Its construction used the soil taken from the field to build up the ring walls and then poured concrete formed the surfaces. This photo was taken from an airplane at the Yale versus Harvard football game on November 20, 1920. *Photographed by Bell Keough. Courtesy of Colin M. Caplan.*

and is to be built in a hole that is to be excavated to a depth of 27 feet, thus making a total of 54 feet from bottom to top. The dimensions of the concrete structure will be 945 feet long by 745 feet in width. Within this will be the oval field 500 by 300 feet in dimensions. It is calculated for a seating capacity of 61,000—larger by far than that of any similar structure in the world, ancient or modern. Whilst it is said that the Coliseum in ancient Rome held some 200,000 people, its real seating capacity did not exceed 50,000. So with the stadium at Athens, the seating capacity was not above 30,000. It is to be remembered that the seating accommodations in these great amphitheaters were only intended for aristocracy, the multitude being provided for with "standing room only."

Access to the Bowl is provided for by two large tunnels and to the seats by thirty smaller tunnels. A drainage system is employed to remove all water from the bottom, and ample provision is also made for supplying water for all purposes. The plans provide for grading and preparing the land between the stadium and the river with ramp-work, driveways and parking spaces for automobiles.

A total of 250,000 cubic yards of dirt must be excavated for the stadium. The Sperry Co. has so far averaged to move 1,000 yards per day. This average includes time spent in preparatory work and has been reached with hand-work only. Machinery is now arriving for the application of steam power to the work. With this installed, a hole of enormous dimensions may be expected to appear before the arrival of cold weather. Charles A. Ferry, Yale '71 S.S.S., was the designer of the Bowl.

SOLDIER'S MEMORIAL GATEWAY

Saturday Chronicle, July 10, 1915

Work has been started on the Westville soldiers' memorial gateway and the monument to the village's national heroes will be completed, it is expected, during the present month. Soon after its completion there will be adequate dedicatory ceremonies. The effort to perpetuate the memory of soldiers of Westville was begun about thirty-five years ago. It will be recalled that about 1880 there broke over the Northern states a wave of patriotism that manifested itself in a frenzy of monument making. Westville, in common

New roads opened through undeveloped land during the mid-nineteenth century. This view shows Edgewood Road in 1869, which Donald Grant Mitchell opened to the public through his Edgewood estate in 1863. After Mitchell's death, the road became what is now called Edgewood Way. *Photographed by Rockwood. Courtesy of Colin M. Caplan.*

Austin Street as seen from the corner of Blake Street, circa 1906, was a quintessential village street. The small neighborhood that developed here in the mid-nineteenth century supplied housing for the local mills, located only a short walk in any direction. *Photographed by T.S. Bronson. Courtesy of the New Haven Museum & Historical Society.*

Looking north on Emerson Street from the corner of Whalley Avenue on December 18, 1908. West Rock looms in the background. Its hard stone was used for building blocks and crushed to pave the streets. The rock became one of the city's first parks in 1889 and is now the second largest state park in Connecticut. *Photographed by T.S. Bronson. Courtesy of the New Haven Museum & Historical Society.*

with the other communities, formed an association for the purpose of making a soldiers' monument, which resulted in the sum of $200 being collected. The money was made a fund that was to be added to from time to time, until it became sufficient to provide the proposed memorial. It would appear that time had dimmed the ardor of the village patriots, for after depositing the money in a savings bank, no further action has been taken for about thirty-five years.

But, when the members of Westville's very efficient civic association learned of the fund a few weeks ago, the realization of a dream more than a quarter of a century old was assured.

On inquiry it was learned that the $200 had grown to, by interest accumulation, about $900. The soldiers' memorial association was spurred on to action and with the selection of Reverend C.F. Luther as president and Mr. George X.X. Crane as secretary, action was immediately begun. Architect Fred Von Beren produced a very handsome and fitting design, which the accompanying illustration inadequately represents.

The design, a Gothic motif, will be executed in a combination of trap rock—the local material—and limestone style for the caps, copings and other ornamental features.

MURDER AND MAYHEM

SERIOUS ACCIDENT

New Haven Palladium, June 6, 1867

A driver of a horse car named Woliver was injured yesterday by being caught between his car and the stone wall of the bridge over the creek just this side of Westville. He was leaning over the side of the car, forgetful of the bridge, when the accident happened. The horses went on and drew the car over the bridge, rolling him around and around between the car and the wall. He was carried home.

> *This accident happened on Whalley Avenue at the bridge over the West River. At the time, the stone arch bridge had stone walls along the sides. A little over two years later, on October 4, 1869, this bridge would be destroyed by a major flood. As for the injured horse driver, the paper reports on him a couple days later.*

New Haven Palladium, June 8, 1867

The horse driver Woliver, injured at the Westville bridge, is recovering.

> *Hamilton Park was privately owned and located just to the east of Edgewood Park, running from Whalley Avenue to Edgewood Avenue. Although the park was located outside of what was considered Westville, the park's usual races and games were associated with the town based on its proximity. The following article describes an unlawful event in the park that clearly struck the ire of the reporter.*

BRUTAL SCENE AT HAMILTON PARK

New Haven Palladium, March 16, 1870

An outrageous affair occurred about ten o'clock last night within the city limits, being no less than a prize fight at Hamilton Park between one White of Bridgeport and one Maloney, bartender at the Shakespeare saloon in Congress Avenue.

About sixty roughs and loungers were present, who, we regret to say, separated without any disturbance among themselves, an occurrence as much to be regretted as the fight itself. The mill took place in the large room in the park building and lasted through six rounds, when Maloney was declared the winner. One hundred dollars a side was the prize. The police got wind of the fight about eleven o'clock and were about to start for the park when they learned that it was over. We hope the participants will be arrested and punished, if such a thing is possible.

The gateway to Hamilton Park once stood along Whalley Avenue opposite Osborn Avenue. This view from a glass-plate slide from around 1900 shows its curious design. The park, originally a private park called Brewster Park in 1859, was the scene of various sporting events, including the first programmed football game between Yale and Columbia. The park also attracted more rough types, like the fight on the eve of March 15, 1870. *Courtesy of Colin M. Caplan.*

Blacksmith's Daughter Burned

New Haven Palladium, March 28, 1870

A daughter of Mr. Martin, the blacksmith of Westville, seven or eight years of age, had a narrow escape from being severely burned the other day while playing with some refuse matches in the yard attached to Wheeler & Beecher's factory. Patrick Carroll, an employee at the almshouse, was passing by, heard her screams and, finding the girl's clothes on fire, put a shawl around her and smothered the flames, burning his own hands severely by doing so.

> *Wheeler & Beecher Company was one of the largest producers of sulphur-tipped matches in the country at this time. This accident must have made them aware of the dangers of leaving their scraps out where kids could pick them up and play with them.*

A Small Tornado

New Haven Register, April 15, 1884

A small tornado visited Westville about eleven o'clock yesterday morning, the atmospheric disturbance commencing near Sherman Warner's residence on Blake Street and following the course of Wintergreen brook for about four hundred yards. Outside the path of the windstorm there was no unusual breeze. A wagon that two men were washing at the brook was lifted from the ground and carried along about twenty feet. A number of limbs were wrenched from the trees bordering the brook. The blow made a noise like the rumbling of heavy wagons over a stone pavement.

> *At nine o'clock on the night of April 23, 1896, an explosion rocked Major George E. Albee's house at 27 Barnett Street, now number 80. The major, his wife and three daughters were home at the time. Major Albee was involved in the raids against Apache Chief Geronimo in the mountains of Mexico at least ten years before. At the time of the bombing, Albee was the rifle practice inspector for the Connecticut National Guard. The site of the house is now an apartment building.*

The Dynamite Fiend

New Haven Evening Register, April 24, 1896

The sudden introduction in New Haven of dynamite as an expression of ill will and murderous intent requires the closest attention of the police department. We do not urge this view as a suspicion that the attempt upon the property and the lives of Major Albee and his family last evening will be carelessly treated by the proper authorities, but because the unauthorized use of dynamite or any similar explosive for any purpose whatever should become the most serious of all the responsibilities that confront the department.

The dastardly wrecking of Major Albee's home last evening was viciously planned but it was clumsily executed. It was no expert in the use and explosive possibilities of dynamite who carried the murderous design into effect. It was a common rascal, moved doubtless by a fancied grievance against his victim, ignorant of how to carry out his purpose and strangely stupid in all the details of his undertaking. We say "strangely stupid" because had the fiend been equal to such an assault he would have been successful in it. If this, therefore, is the correct diagnosis of the spirit of the person the authorities are looking for, it ought to be comparatively easy to trace him to his place of concealment. And in this undertaking, Major Albee himself ought to be of the greatest assistance to the police.

We want this fiend captured and punished. It won't do to encourage the careless use of bombs, and it won't do to treat leniently the miscreant when found. It ought not to count in his favor a hair's breadth that the stupidly planned blow failed of its object. He ought to be incarcerated for the rest of his natural days, or for a sufficient long term of years to give him time to meditate and to encourage meditation in others. No stone should be left unturned to track this villain out, and if a handsome reward is necessary to interest others the mayor of the city ought to offer it at once.

The following series of articles tell the story about an intense murder mystery. A body was found in a wooded area and all the clues led back to a man who had been seen at a local saloon, then called the Edgewood Hotel, later the site of the Cape Codder and presently the site of Delaney's. A series of shocking events led to the culprit's arrest and more details about his ill ways were revealed.

Westville Scene of Murder Case; Man Found Shot

New Haven Evening Register, April 3, 1913
Resident on the way to Business Finds Body in Bushes—Others Heard Two Shots During Night—Identity of Victim Not Positive.

Baffles Officials

Lying in a pool of blood, a man supposed to be Patrick Donahue, formerly employed by the city in the street department and also an ex-watchman at one of the icehouses in Westville, was found in a cluster of bushes in a secluded spot just off Tryon Street, Westville, halfway between Central and Whalley Avenue about 6:30 this morning with a wound from a .32-caliber revolver in the back of his head.

The Westville authorities are at a loss to account for a motive for the murder, although one of the man's vest pockets was turned inside out and nothing was found in his pockets save a five-cent piece. The murdered man is known to have been drinking yesterday afternoon and early last night. The Westville police and the local detectives have been called into the case by Coroner Mix and are probing every clue to the identity of the murderer.

There was nothing on the man's person that would disclose his identity, but several Westville people say they recognized him as Patrick Donahue, about forty-five years old, who was well known in that locality.

Found at 6:30 O'clock

The body was found about 6:30 o'clock this morning by Charles Hildreth of Burton Street, Westville. Mr. Hildreth was on his way to work this morning at the Winchester Repeating Arms Company when he noticed the body of a man. The man's head, face and neck were covered with blood and Mr. Hildreth hurried to the home of Policeman Dingwall, about two hundred feet away, and notified him of the discovery.

Policemen D.M. Ahern and Dingwall started an investigation after Medical Examiner Scarborough was called, and the probe brought to light the fact that the bushes in the immediate vicinity of the place where the body was found were all bent over, some freshly broken, and footsteps in the soft turf made it appear as though at least three persons had been tramping near that spot during the night or early morning.

The body was found at the bottom of a hill about thirty feet high, which is known as the Mix grounds. From the top of the hill to the bottom, where the body lay, there were irregular footsteps, which leads the authorities to believe that the man was at the top of the hill and he was then shot and either pushed or fell down the hill.

Facts that support the theory that a hard scuffle took place on the top of the hill were that the bushes on the top in a direct line with the footsteps on the hill were bent over and broken a great deal more than they could possibly have been by even several persons wading through them.

In looking about the place, Policeman Ahern picked up a razor that was about ten feet from the body. The razor was closed and unstained, giving the Westville police the impression that one of the men of the supposed three had either dropped it or that it belonged to the dead man and had fallen out of his clothes.

HEARD SHOTS

Roy Welch, a grocery clerk in the employ of his father, P.J. Welch, and James Cousins, a friend, told the police that they were sitting on a stairway at 845 Whalley Avenue this morning about 12:35 o'clock when they heard two reports of either a revolver or gun. They declared that they paid little attention to the reports, but remembered they came from the direction of where the body was found.

The remains were taken to the undertaking rooms of Lewis & Maycock, where instructions have been left by Medical Examiner Scarborough not to let anyone touch the body or even see the body for the present, as an autopsy will soon be performed in an effort to shed some light on the mystery.

The man wore a derby hat, with a mark indicating that it was purchased at Lambert's. The hat was about eight feet from the body and lay on the ground in a flat position. There were several dents in the top of the hat. He wore a brown overcoat about knee length, which had a Waterbury tailor's signature, and he wore blue trousers, blue coat and new black shoes.

This afternoon the police learned that a man resembling the one found dead went into a Westville saloon and asked for a drink, but that he was intoxicated and it was refused by John McConville, the bartender.

The Westville police late this afternoon secured the information that the dead man was in the Edgewood hotel, 892 Whalley Avenue, for some time last evening in company with a young man described as being about twenty-five years of age. The two, according to the saloonkeeper, had a number of drinks in the hotel and left about 11:40. As they left the saloon, Donohue ordered a quart of whiskey and in paying for it pulled out a roll of bills and paid a dollar for the liquor. The two then left the hotel.

The young man is described as being about twenty-five years of age, and wore an overcoat, black derby hat and tan shoes.

Song and Dance Man Slayer in Westville Murder?

New Haven Evening Register, April 4, 1913
Edgewood Hotel Proprietor Recalls Presence of Pair in His Place Shortly Before Shooting—Nearly Shot a Man in Afternoon, Youth Boasted

The police and detectives investigating the supposed murder that occurred in Westville early yesterday morning now believe that the actual shooting took place about one hundred feet from where the body of the unknown dead man was found, and that he was either dragged or that he staggered and dropped some distance away. The authorities feel certain that a young man seen with the dead man will soon be apprehended.

The remains, which have been viewed by hundreds of people, are yet unidentified, although several persons who saw the deceased and the younger man in his company during the night before last heard the younger of the two refer to him as "Pop" and also as "Pat Donohue."

P.P. Sperry Jr., proprietor of the Edgewood Hotel in Whalley Avenue, Westville, gave the authorities information that has developed good clues as far as the identity of the suspected young man, who was last seen in company with the accused. When interviewed this morning, Mr. Sperry said:

> About quarter past eleven the night before last, I was tending bar and the man who was found dead walked into my place in company with a young man about twenty-five years old. The young man wore a derby hat that was tilted slightly to one side. He was of medium height, had long black hair, which was especially long, wore no overcoat, but had on a blue or black suit.
>
> The man who was found shot walked up to the middle of the bar and bought two drinks. He called for beer and gave one to his younger friend. They had not finished drinking the beer when the younger fellow said,

"Say Pop, we need some whiskey don't you think so?" The older man then leaned over the bar and asked me for a pint of whiskey. I gave it to him and the older man paid me thirty-five cents. He had some more change, but that he put back in his pocket.

At that moment the young fellow turned around and looking at several men in the place said, "I suppose you guys don't think I can sing and dance. Well I can, but I have to be pretty well oiled up first. I guess I was in good condition to sing and dance this afternoon, for we were thrown out of four different places in the city. Wasn't we Pop?"

"Say Pop, before I start I want to thank you for what you did for me this afternoon. Do you know that only for you I would have blown off that -- -- nigger's head in that last place. I wouldn't stand for anyone calling me a -- -- --. Yes I would have plugged him right only for you," he continued.

While he was saying that I saw him feel of his hip pocket several times, but I didn't become suspicious in the least at that time. But I'll tell you one thing I could pick that fellow out of a thousand. I could tell him in a minute. He seemed to me with his long black hair as what we sometimes call a "hard guy." Well, anyway, after a while he started to sing. He started with "Sweet Adeline." Just at the time the older man said: "That's the song you were singing all afternoon. It's no wonder we got put out of four places." The older man turned away, evidently trying to make the young man think he was disgusted with the singing when the young man suddenly stopped and said: "Why I've sung in nicolets. I've danced in them, too, and if I got by all right before hundreds of people there, well I certainly can in a barroom. Drink it up and come on Pop. We better be beating it."

The two men left the place about 11:40 o'clock and were seen walking from the Edgewood Hotel toward Tryon Street, where the bullet-punctured body of the older man was later found.

Detective Sergeant Ward, who is working on the case, picked up a suspect this morning in a Fair Street saloon who resembled the man with the long hair who was seen last with the dead man. After a grilling, the police became satisfied that he wasn't the man who was in the saloon with the unknown dead man and he was released.

Coroner Mix this morning declared that no material developments have shown up as yet and they are at a loss as far as the motive for the supposed murder can be. As was stated in yesterday's *Register*, one of the vest pockets of the dead man was found turned inside out and only one five-cent piece was found in his clothes. A Westville man who was in the Edgewood Hotel when the pair walked in this morning insisted that he was positive that he saw the older man take a gold watch out of his pocket and look at the time on several different occasions. When his body was discovered, no watch was found in his clothes.

The authorities are convinced that the bullet that entered the dead man's head was fired at close range, although not close enough to lead the police to believe it was self-inflicted. Today the police secured the vicinity of the woods and roadway for a great distance all around.

The autopsy of the body has not yet been performed but will take place probably late this afternoon.

Sharing the front page with the preceding article was the following article, which by all accounts seemed unrelated. But the violence-fueled actions of one man over a few days would soon be revealed.

Kobie Lawler Shot Twice by Man in Bank

New Haven Evening Register, April 4, 1913
Detective Wounded Twice as He Takes Man as Forger—Is Rushed to Hospital in Serious Condition.

Detective Sergeant Edward F. Lawler, better known as "Kobie" Lawler, was shot twice in the head by a William Allen, who he was taking out of the New Haven County National Bank this afternoon, and is now at St. Raphael's Hospital in a serious condition.

He was summoned there by the officials of the bank, who called the police station and said that they were detaining the man there. Detective Lawler hastened over and took charge of the man. Starting to leave the bank on the way to headquarters, the man drew a revolver and shot the detective twice in the head. Detective Lawler fell to the floor of the bank unconscious and the man started to run out of the building.

The shooting, coming at the busiest part of the day caused a tremendous excitement in the vicinity of the bank.

The man is a heroin victim, it is said. The man made a pretense of drawing his handkerchief from his pocket, but instead drew a revolver and fired pointblank at the detective. Four of the shots took effect. Lawler did not fall but as he staggered was assisted by a couple of bystanders to the drugstore on the corner.

The man ran diagonally across the street, where he was caught by two men who had been attracted by the shots. He made no attempt to escape. The identity of the man who fired the shots was determined at headquarters. He is William Allen, employed on the railroad as an assistant. He lived in Bridgeport and is between thirty and thirty-seven years of age.

Detective Lawler has been connected with the police department for a long period, and was quite successful in doing "plain clothes" duty downtown, which meritorious work eventually landed him in the detective department. He is always good natured and humorous, but nevertheless keen and a terror to the evil-doers of the lower section of the city.

IDENTIFY ALLEN AS ONE WHO WAS WITH SLAIN MAN

New Haven Evening Register, April 5, 1913
Lawler Laughs at His Narrow Escape

The condition of Detective Kobie Lawler was much improved this morning. He was sitting in the parlor of his home at 24 Market Street, his wounds being dressed by Dr. Seymour L. Spier, the police surgeon.

"I'm the luckiest guy who ever lived," laughed the detective this morning. "I saw the gun being pushed up in front of me and could have avoided being shot by letting go, but I held on to him. I felt my face burn all of a sudden following a report. There was a stinging sensation in my cheek and I knew I was shot. I tried to push the point of the revolver the other way, but I wouldn't have let him go unless he shot my hands off," continued the sleuth.

Three Westville Citizens Declare Man Who Tried to Kill "Kobie" Lawler Was With Victim of Foul Play in Saloon Just Before Shooting.

EXPECT A CONFESSION
Although stoutly professing his innocence as far as being responsible for the Westville murder is concerned, William Allen, a locomotive fireman who

shot and painfully wounded Detective "Kobie" Lawler yesterday afternoon, was this morning identified by three different persons as the man who was in the Edgewood Hotel barroom in Westville with the murdered man a few hours before the murder. After being brought before the body in the undertaking rooms, where he was grilled, he finally admitted he was with the man who was later found dead but that he didn't "do the trick," as he expressed himself.

From eight o'clock yesterday afternoon until twelve o'clock last night, Coroner Mix and the detectives gave Allen their "third degree," and at eleven o'clock this morning he was again taken into the Bertillon room, where the grilling was reopened. Every known method was used to wring a confession from the man, but according to late reports this was not forthcoming, although one of the detectives stated afterward that he was "softening."

Those who positively identified Allen as the man who was with the dead man at the Edgewood Hotel about a half hour before the man was murdered are P.P. Sperry Jr., proprietor of the hotel; Albert Lyman, who rooms at the house; and George Clock, twenty-one years old of Blake Street, Westville. Those men, one by one, were led before Detective Lawler and without the slightest hesitation accused Allen of being with the man who claimed he was a song and dance actor in the Edgewood Hotel.

Yesterday afternoon about four o'clock young Clock was led into the Bertillon room, where the prisoner was sitting. As soon as Clock opened the door, Allen began to appear uneasy, and Clock, after looking a moment at the accused, smiled and said, "So you're the song and dance artist, are you?"

Allen tried to rise from the chair but was pushed back by a detective and he shouted, "Who the --- are you? What's your name and where do you live?"

"You know me," said Clock. "Why didn't you sing 'Sweet Adeline' in the Edgewood Hotel in Westville the other night about twenty minutes to twelve?"

"You're a liar," snapped Allen. "I never was in Westville."

After Clock was excused, Mr. Sperry and Lyman were both brought before the man, and like Clock told the authorities that they were sure Allen was the man they had seen in the hotel.

Allen had little if any sleep last night and he called constantly for cocaine. Despite the reports regarding Allen not being a "bing fiend," Captain of Police Thomas Dunn this morning declared that when brought in yesterday afternoon, Allen stated that he was a "bing fiend." To support that fact, Allen cried for cocaine every few minutes last night, but the police believe he is just "stalling" and that he is not really afflicted with the habit. However, the police did not call a physician.

P.P. Sperry Jr., proprietor of the Edgewood Hotel, this morning in an interview said: "It was just as I said yesterday. I could pick that fellow out of a thousand. Why, when he was in here with the older man Wednesday night he walked up to me and he said, 'I know you, Sperry. You're the guy who trimmed me once. You beat me up about three years ago. Do you remember? Well, anyway, I ordered a sandwich in this place and I didn't have nickel to pay for it. You threw me out and beat me pretty bad, but that's years ago and we'll forget that now.'

"It was on that account," continued Mr. Sperry, "that I paid a good deal of attention to him and yesterday when I saw him, I knew he was the man. I told him right in front of his face that he was the fellow, and he called me different names."

Allen, the accused, is a nephew of James A. Allen, a milkman of 399 Central Avenue, Westville. He is the son of Minot Allen, who with his family moved from Westville to Bridgewell, Delaware.

Allen also was employed at the Weber farm in Woodbridge about five years ago and suddenly disappeared after an argument with a hired man to whose bed he set fire. The hired man was badly burned and Allen at the time left Woodbridge and joined the United States Army, from which he later deserted. He was not seen about Westville until two years later, when he had trouble with Mr. Sperry.

The arrest of Allen came about in a peculiar way. Yesterday afternoon about one o'clock, Allen entered the saloon of Carbino & Migliozzi at 78 Fair Street. He had been drinking heavily. In the afternoon he began talking with several persons and walked up to the bar and, without putting any money down, asked for another drink. He was refused and he shouted, "Refuse me, will you? Well, I could make you come across if I felt like it; don't you think I couldn't. You think you are in a class with the people in this country, and if someone placed all of you in boats and then sank the boats a --- of a lot of harm wouldn't be done. I'd like to pepper a few of you myself, so come along, hand over a drink!"

The bartender then became suspicious of Allen and for the purpose of keeping peace for a while, gave him a glass of beer. He then slipped out and telephoned to detective headquarters, stating that a suspicious man was in the saloon. The bartender asked that Detective Gianelli be sent, but as Gianelli was on another case at the time, Detective Lawler was assigned to the case. Detective Lawler went to the place and when he arrived there he found that Allen had left. Hurrying out, he spied Allen entering another saloon and walked up to him and grabbed him by the arm, telling him that he was a detective and that he was under arrest.

"What for?" shouted Allen.

"Never mind now. The captain wants to see you, that's all," answered Detective Lawler.

Evidently laboring under the impression that Detective Lawler wanted him for the Westville murder, Allen whipped out a revolver in State Street, near Chapel Street, and fired it five times at the detective. One of the shots entered Detective Lawler's left cheek and went out his face, passing just under his ear. Another shot scraped his forehead, while another tore its way through the padding of his coat.

Allen has constantly been calling for cigarettes, which he was allowed quite frequently since arrested. Yesterday afternoon, when first grilled, he repeatedly said, "I wish I had killed him. I'm as good as he is," he repeated.

Allen is at present charged with assault with intent to kill, for which a bond of $5,000 was fixed by Judge Hoyt in the city court this morning. The fixing of the bond was simply a matter of form, for he is being held by the coroner without bonds in connection with the Westville murder.

Captain of Detectives Donnelley, who supervised with Coroner Mix the grill of the accused, this morning stated that he had just learned Allen is wanted on a serious charge in Boston or Springfield, but declared that he would not go into the details any further at this time.

The positive identification of the murdered man in Westville has not yet been made, although hundreds of people have called daily at the rooms of Lewis & Maycock for that purpose. It is now believed that his home has recently been in Hartford. The only motive the police claim as the reason for the murder by Allen is robbery. Allen at one time lived at 394 Dixwell Avenue and lately 301 Dixwell Avenue. Allen was taken to jail this afternoon and the grilling will take place again, the authorities feeling confident that a confession by Allen will soon be forthcoming.

ALLEN, CONFESSING, GOES OVER SCENE OF WESTVILLE CRIME

New Haven Journal-Courier, April 7, 1913
Succumbs to Long Grilling and Admits Guilt, Detectives Intimate—Taken to Tryon Street for Purpose of Rehearsing Details of Killing

Victim Unidentified

That William B. Allen, the would-be slayer of Detective "Kobie" Lawler, confessed to having murdered the unidentified man in a secluded spot in Tryon Street, Westville, was the intimation of the authorities just at twelve o'clock this noon when the morning grilling ended. Allen was handcuffed to Detective Sergeant Ward, led into an awaiting automobile and, with Coroner Mix and Captain Donnelly, was rushed to Westville and brought to the spot in Tryon Street where the dead body of the unknown man was found early Thursday morning.

The authorities refused to give out any of the confession for publication at this time but there is little doubt that Allen broke down under the long grill and told all. Just as Captain Donnelly was climbing into the automobile, before it started on the way to Westville, he said when asked regarding the confession: "It's all over; that's all I have to say now. He's the man."

When the party arrived at Tryon Street, Westville, Allen was led out of the automobile and taken to the spot where the body was found. There he kept pointing to the place, and at the hill and at the roads approaching the spot. It was learned early this afternoon that he showed the police where the whiskey bottle, which the two men had, was cast away.

One report this afternoon was that Allen declared he was fooling with the revolver and jokingly pointed it at the dead man in Tryon street about 100 feet away from where the body was later found. He said according to the report that the instant the unknown man saw the revolver he made a grab for it, and he accidentally touched Allen's finger and the gun discharged.

That report had it that Allen attempted to cover up the case until he got a distance away and so he dragged the body to the spot it was originally found and cast it into the bushes. He then climbed the hill and left. That report, which was discussed in police circles, could not be verified, but the fact nevertheless that Allen confessed to have shot the unknown was true, for Coroner Mix was later asked if he would deny that "Allen confessed," and he replied to the negative.

Deep mystery still enshrouds the identity of the murdered victim. Many local people viewed his remains yesterday and today, and a large number thought the features of the dead man compared closely with someone they knew, but they couldn't think just who it was.

William B. Allen was indicted for first-degree murder in the killing of the unidentified man, later found to be Francis P. Cunningham. He pleaded not guilty.

Motorman Hit by Mix Report

New Haven Journal-Courier, December 16, 1914
Coroner Suggests He Was Not Alert Enough in Whalley Avenue Crash—No Blame Criminally—Recommendation for Slowdown Signal Is Complied with At Once.

Although he finds that Giuseppe Moccia, killed by collision with a trolley car on Whalley Avenue, Westville, on December 10, did not come to his death on account of the criminal negligence of anyone, Coroner Eli Mix, in his official finding made yesterday, says that, in his opinion, the motorman of the car that collided with Moccia's wagon was not alert and was not keeping a good lookout just previous to, and at the time the collision happened. He has advised that a slowdown signal be installed by the Connecticut Company at the point where the collision occurred, at the intersection of West Fitch Street and Whalley Avenue, on account of the steep grade at that spot that accelerates the momentum of double truck cars. Vice-president John K. Punderford, of the Connecticut Company, stated last night that in conformity with the recommendation, he had already ordered a "slowdown signal" to be placed at once at that point.

The full text of the coroner's report on the fatality is as follows:

> Having been notified on the tenth day of December, A.D. 1914, that Giuseppe Moccia, a white male, eighteen years of age, late of the town and county of New Haven, state of Connecticut, had come to a violent death in said town of New Haven, I at once made immediate inquiry concerning the manner and cause of said death. After said inquiry and having reason to suspect said death was caused by the criminal act, omission or carelessness of another or others, I held an inquest as to the manner and cause of said death.
>
> Deceased boarded at 8 Locust street, and was employed as a teamster by Michele A. Adinolfi, 404 East street, who delivers coal for the W.F. Gilbert Coal company. He had been a teamster for a number of months past. Shortly after 6 p.m., December 10th, 1914, while returning from Westville where he had been delivering coal with a heavy coal cart to which was attached two horses he was driving easterly upon the southerly side of Whalley avenue where are located trolley tracks of the Connecticut company. When in the vicinity of West Fitch street which intersects said

avenue on its northerly side, car No. 549 of said company was going westerly on its run towards Westville, and car No. 610 of said company was proceeding easterly on its run towards the city, both being equipped with small incandescent headlights.

As west bound car No. 549 was about opposite West Fitch street, it collided with said team, throwing the horses and fore wheels upon the east bound track over and against the left front vestibule of car No. 610, which had reached said point and was about to pass car No. 549. By reason of said collision the vestibule of car No. 549 was completely wrecked, the left front vestibule of car No. 610 was also wrecked and deceased was thrown from his team into the wreckage of vestibule of car No. 549, causing his immediate death.

I find as approach is made westerly in this locality, there is a descending grade of $4\frac{1}{2}$ per cent of the highway and tracks for a considerable distance; that there is an electric light at the corner of Jewel street which intersects said highway on its northerly side and is the first street east of West Fitch street, that there is a gas light at said West Fitch street; that the night was clear, and with the headlight with which said car No. 549 was equipped, objects could be seen about one hundred feet ahead.

It is stated by said motorman of car No. 549 that he was about eight feet away when he first observed said team on his track; that he sounded his gong; that deceased turned his horses to the left toward the incoming track, but it is apparent from the appearance of the vestibule of his car and the complete wreckage of the heavy cart that his car collided with said team with great force, and I am of the opinion said motorman, William McLaughlin, was not alert and was not keeping a good look-out just previous to and at the time said collision occurred.

I find that while deceased was driving upon the tracks of said company, it not being necessary at the time for him to do so, for the reason that the highway in this locality is of considerable width and was entirely clear of traffic, yet under the conditions that existed, I am of the opinion said motorman of said west bound car No. 549 should have been able to see the team of said deceased a sufficient distance away to have checked the speed of his car which at the time was going at a moderate rate, and to have brought his car to a stop before striking the same, thus avoiding the accident.

Owing to the steep grade existing in the vicinity where the collision occurred which with the momentum of heavy double truck cars is conducive to high speed, I am of the opinion a "slow down" signal should be installed by said company at this locality, and I recommend that this be done.

I am satisfied that said death was not caused by the criminal act or carelessness of any person or persons.

Dated at New Haven, Conn., this 14th day of December, 1914, upon which date I filed with the desk of the superior court for New Haven county my report of the inquest, together with the testimony taken thereat.

Eli Mix.
Coroner for New Haven County

Death on West Rock

New Haven Evening Register, March 7, 1915

Since finding Lillian Cook on the top of West Rock Thursday afternoon, many residents have told of the different ones who have met their deaths on West Rock. There seems to be a peculiar fascination about the rock for those who contemplate suicide. It seems a pity that it should be so, for it is such a magnificent spot naturally and with the aid of man in the last decade has been even improved. It now has beautiful drives and attractive footpaths.

A year ago this time a young woman named Mrs. August Erikson, wife of a high school instructor, was found frozen to death at the base of the rock. It was just below the path leading out of the park to the spring. Some young school boys accidentally discovered her while at play on the "island" nearby. About three years ago a Yale student, unbalanced from overstudy, threw himself over the face of the rock and was discovered by two other students. Many Yale students have tried to climb the face of the rock and some have lost their lives in the attempt. People who have climbed the Alps in Switzerland always feel a desire to ascend the face of West Rock.

Yesterday and Friday any number of visitors walked up the rock to view the spot where the body of the missing girl was discovered.

FLAMES DO $20,000 DAMAGE TO SPERRY PROPERTY IN WESTVILLE

New Haven Evening Register, November 28, 1921
Blaze Detected in Old Elm Tree Inn by Trolley Crew Keeps Tired Firemen at Work Through Early Morning

Fire, which did damage to the extent of some $20,000, rendered three families homeless and caused injuries from smoke to six firemen to such an extent that they had to be taken to Grace Hospital for treatment, broke out in the property of Pearl B. Sperry in Westville, at the junction of Whalley Avenue, Central Avenue and Fountain Street.

The threatened danger was first noticed by the crew of the "Owl" trolley, Thomas Mangan, conductor, and John Saars, motorman, who noticed a wreath of smoke ascending the building, which is a frame construction of two stories, as they were about to make their trip to the city. While one of the men rang in an alarm on box 3312, the other soon joined by his partner, woke up three families lying in the upper part of the building, by which time the blaze had assumed threatening proportions. However, it was found possible to allow families time to obtain clothes before leaving their homes for the street and by this time the fire department had arrived on the scene. At first it appeared as the though the fire was one that might be overcome by use of a chemical, but as soon as the blaze was extinguished in one spot it broke out into another until finally a second alarm was sent in, bringing all the apparatus from the western end of the city.

The blaze was a stubborn one and it was not before daylight that the place was regarded as safe from further destruction, and in the meanwhile the upper floor of the building had been practically destroyed, with contents. The ground floor, occupied on the Central Avenue side by the Edgewood Garage, distributors of the Larrabee truck, at the corner of Whalley Avenue and Central Avenue by the Economy grocery company, and on the Whalley Avenue side by a vacant store formerly a restaurant, suffered severely from smoke and water, although no actual fire damage was done to these premises.

The origin of the fire is unknown but is generally thought to be the result of crossed electric wires, or possibly caused by rats either through electric wires or matches. It seems to have started in a partition on the Central Avenue side and worked its way throughout the entire upper floor in spite of the endeavors of the firemen to confine it to one spot.

The families who occupied the upper floor were those of David W. Smith, Charles A. Bell and Frank Mullen, and as soon as it became apparent that their homes were in danger, Pearl B. Sperry, owner of the property, with his own home in the next house west, threw open his doors to his tenants, and Mr. Sperry's home this morning had the appearance of a small hotel in concentrated form. Most of the personal belongings of the three families were, however, saved, although there was no opportunity to salvage furniture.

The site of the fire is one of considerable local interest, standing as it does where the old "Elm Tree" Inn once stood, a hostelry famous for many years. The premises as they stood yesterday were erected by Mr. Sperry some ten years ago and were of two-story construction, with stores on the entrance floor.

The reporter was in fact misinformed about the original location of this building. The Elm Tree Inn was located in the next block east, across Central Avenue, torn down around 1910. The site of Mr. Sperry's building was an inn called the Hotel Edgewood. The building was originally two separate buildings, the one on the corner of Central Avenue originally the old central district school called Franklin Hall, built on Harrison Street around 1830. The school was moved around 1870 to Fountain Street and then moved here in 1880, next to an existing house of the same vintage. In 1913, Mr. Sperry hired New Haven architect Charles E. Joy to design a uniform Classical façade through additions and alterations. The building was fixed after the fire and still houses apartments on the upper floors and a restaurant and tavern on the bottom.

THE GRAND ESTATES

Two large estates dominated Westville's late nineteenth- and early twentieth-century landscape. They were owned by two men who cared for the rural, pastoral nature that existed on the fringes of town at that time. Donald Grant Mitchell, a prolific author of some fame whose pen name was Ik Marvel, purchased an estate named Rosebank in 1858. He renamed it Edgewood and developed and nurtured the estate's rough edges, building a new rustic-style house around 1870, co-designed by New Haven architect and friend

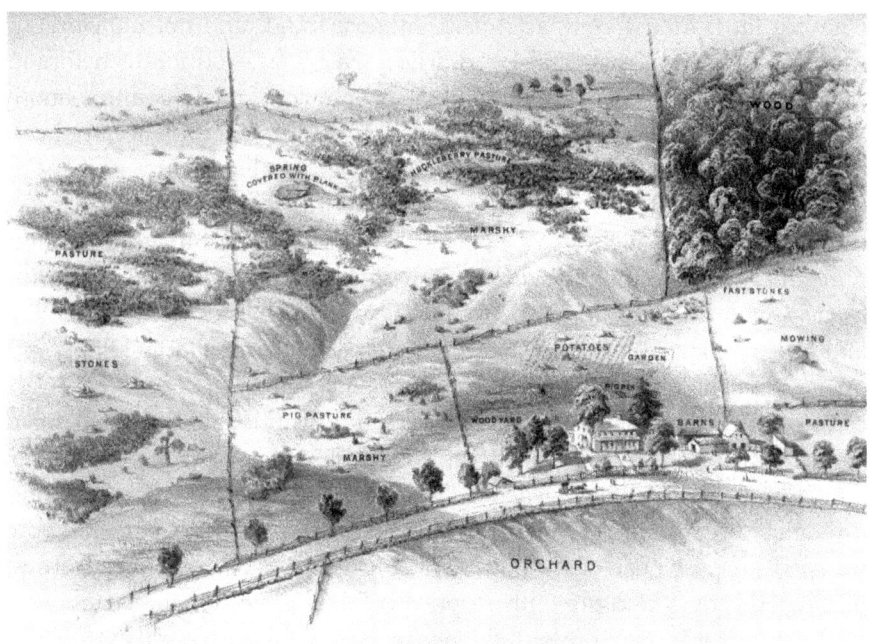

Edgewood homestead at date of purchase. This bird's-eye map shows the Edgewood Estate at the time that Donald Grant Mitchell purchased it in 1858. The original farm, called Rosebank, was built and developed by Isaac Dickerman in the mid-eighteenth century. *Drawn by Donald Grant Mitchell. Courtesy of Colin M. Caplan.*

David R. Brown. The Edgewood estate spanned from Edgewood Park west into the woody hillside. The following is an excerpt from Mitchell's own literary dedication to Edgewood that describes his first experience of the estate.

Approach from the North

Pictures of Edgewood, 1869
By Donald G. Mitchell

It seems but yesterday that I drove from among the tasteful houses of the town, which since my boy-time had crept far out upon the margin of the plain. It seems to me that I can recall the note of an oriole that sung gushingly from the limbs of an overreaching elm as we passed. I know I remember the stately, broad road we took, and its smooth, firm macadam. I have a fancy that I compared it in my own mind, and not unfavorably, with the metal of a road that I had driven over only two months before in the environs of Liverpool. I remember a somewhat stately country house that we passed, whose architecture dissolved any illusions I might have been under in regard to my whereabouts. I remember turning slightly, perhaps to the right, and the threading the ways of a neat little manufacturing village—catching views of waterfalls, of tall chimneys, of open pasture grounds; and remember bridges, and other bridges, and how the village straggled on with its neat white palings and whiter houses, with honeysuckles at the doors, and how we skirted a pond, where the pads of lilies lay all idly afloat; and how a great hulk of rock loomed up suddenly near a thousand feet, with dwarfed cedars and oaks tufting its crevices, tufting its top, and how we drove almost beneath it, so that I seemed to be in Meyringen again, and to hear the dash of the foaming Reichenbach and how we ascended again, drifting through another limb of the village, where the little churches stood; and how we sped on past neat white houses—rising gently—skirted by hedgerows of tangled cedars, and presently stopped before a grayish-white farmhouse, where the air was all aflow with the perfume of great purple spikes of lilacs. And thence—though we had risen so little I had scarce noticed a hill—we saw all the spires of the city we had left, two miles away as a bird flies, and they seemed to stand cushioned on a broad bower of leaves; and to the right of them, where they straggled and faded, there came to the eye a white

A young portrait of famed author, landscape designer and gentleman farmer Donald Grant Mitchell in 1869. Westville's most esteemed resident, Mitchell wrote by the pen name Ik Marvel. He was born in 1822 in eastern Connecticut, graduated Yale College in 1841 and happened upon his Westville estate in 1858. Mitchell became indulged in the land, plants and animals that surrounded his home on Forest Road. *Photographed by Rockwood. Courtesy of Colin M. Caplan.*

burst of water which was an arm of the sea; beyond the harbor and town was a purple hazy range of hills—in the foreground a little declivity, and then a wide plateau of level land, green and lusty with all the wealth of June sunshine. I had excuse to be fastidious in the matter of landscape, for within three months I had driven on Richmond hill, and had luxuriated in the valley-scene from the *côte* of St. Cloud. But neither one nor the other forbade my open and outspoken admiration of the view before me.

I have a recollection of making my way through the hedging lilacs and ringing with nervous haste at the doorbell; and as I turned, the view from the step seemed to me even wider and more enchanting than from the carriage. I have a fancy that a middle-aged man, with iron-gray whiskers, answered my summons in his shirt-sleeves and proposed joining me directly under some trees that stood a little way to the north. I recollect dimly a little county coquetry of his, about unwillingness to sell, or to name a price; and yet how he kindly pointed out to me where his cows were feeding, just southward, and were hemmed in to the north by a heavy belt of timber.

I think we are all hypocrites at a bargain. I suspect I threw out casual objections to the house, and the distance and the roughness; and yet have an uneasy recollection of thanking my friend for having brought to my notice the most charming spot I had yet seen, and one that met my wish in nearly every particular.

It seems to me that the ride to town must have been very short and my dinner a hasty one: I know I have a clear recollection of wandering over those hills, and that plateau of farmland, afoot, that very afternoon. I remember tramping through the wood and testing the turf after the manner of my lank friend upon the Hudson. I can recall distinctly the aspect of house, and hills, as they came into view on my second drive from the town; how a great stretch of forest, which lay in common, flanked the whole, so that the farm could be best and most intelligibly described as—lying on the edge of the wood; and it seemed to me, that, if it should be mine, it should wear the name of—Edgewood.

"IK MARVEL" AT HOME, A VISIT TO THE AUTHOR AT HIS FIRESIDE

Saturday Chronicle, March 22, 1902

With the wind howling at a forty-mile clip, sweeping the sand from the plains at the foot of the hill, ratting the tree tops, snapping the branches, felling some of the big trunks that had gone stale, Donald G. Mitchell, the author, the man who wrote *Reveries of a Bachelor*, even if nothing else, sat before a glowing fireplace in his cheerful library and received a *Saturday Chronicle* man Wednesday afternoon.

Outside all was tempestuous—the gale shook the rafters of old Edgewood, the trees bent and swayed as if they ached, the swirl of dust and hail and sleet made a picture through the window. But it wasn't much of a day for a stroll, even on the well-laid walk leading to Edgewood.

"Well," said Mr. Mitchell, as he drew a chair for the visitor near to the blazing fireplace, "as my daughter perhaps told you, I am not feeling very well today, and I am so much in retirement that I seldom see others than old friends. But a man who comes to me today, through all this blow outside, should be welcomed, I think, and so I am glad to meet you.

"I'm living a quiet life, one might call it a life of seclusion. My companion at present is the open grate, the embers, the birch which does not snap sparks on the rug, the contentment of mind and body which is cherished.

"Your paper, the *Chronicle*, is bright and full of good features, but so far as I am concerned I don't like it; I don't like the idea of having my picture printed in it. I'm not interested, you know, and I encourage ignorance about myself, so far as I can."

The sparkle of the eyes, the heartiness of the handshake, the pictures and the volumes about the walls belied the words. "Ik Marvel," the man who many years ago made young men glad, and who pointed out how they might stay so, had nothing to say at eighty. His fellow aged seventeen, was scarcely referred to. It is the best gift of the maiden to the young man—*The Reveries of a Bachelor*. Perhaps, some day, there will be another "Ik Marvel," but he never will set the pulse and brain agoing just like this "Ik Marvel" did.

"Ik Marvel" is responsible for a good deal, but he has the satisfying thought that it is all on the good side. As a matchmaker he has done more than all the rest, just because he put it the way it is. Others depend upon bluff, cash, opera boxes and the whirl for emphasis. But an appeal to the heart of a true man will any time counterbalance the dead weight on the other end of the teeter. So, "Ik Marvel" won, when the trash went begging. The young man, not yet of age, who hasn't read *Reveries of a Bachelor* has a duty to perform. It will do him good. It's just the right kind of tonic for age seventeen. Don't shake it—sit down, put on a log and read it. Then shut your eyes and reflect.

Mr. Mitchell said,

> Yes, I am a Yale graduate, class of 1841. I was honored by Yale in 1878, when I was in Europe, with the degree of LLD. I was born in New London County, in the country, in 1822. The college library book of the class of '41 will give you what you want, but I don't like the idea of publicity. I'm quiet here and I cannot see how my picture will be of value to anybody. There are about a dozen men who belonged to the class of '41, and I suppose I am one of the oldest graduates. They cross them off when they die, you know. Judge William L. Learned of Albany is one of my classmates.
>
> Yes, I read the papers every day, and have interest in the things that are going on, but I don't care much for the general news. I prefer quietude. *Reveries of a Bachelor* was written in 1852, and my last book was written, I think, in 1893. *American Lands and Letters*. What is the most important novel today? Oh, don't try to interview me—really, you must excuse me. If you should tell me something about the poor people down there, or over there, or back of the hill, or somewhere else, I'd be glad to hear it and do what I could, but you must not interview me, because I'm quiet, and that's all. So, too, must I dismiss the query if there is to be another Hawthorne or Bryant. I cannot say, and certainly not for printing in a newspaper.

Above: Donald Grant Mitchell worked with New Haven architect David R. Brown to design a rustic-style farmhouse around 1860. This view in 1869 shows the house with barns in the background that date from the farm's prior owner. The house eventually became home to Mitchell's daughter, Susan Hoppin Mitchell. *Photographed by Rockwood. Courtesy of Colin M. Caplan.*

Below: A view looking north from the main house at Edgewood farm in 1869 showing Donald Grant Mitchell on the far right-hand side and his wife and daughter in the middle. Mitchell preserved many of the old stands of woods on the property, but he also designed numerous landscape features. Mitchell enjoyed the pastoral quality on his farm and spent much of his later years staying put here. *Photographed by Rockwood. Courtesy of Colin M. Caplan.*

THE GRAND ESTATES   111

Above: The hillside and lawn on Donald Grant Mitchell's Edgewood estate was quite a scene in this 1869 view. Mitchell's wife and daughter look on from a windy path on the left-hand side. The view is looking southwest from Mitchell's main house. The broad, sloping hill was long referred to as Chestnut Hill, and the area is now home to the Hopkins School. *Photographed by Rockwood. Courtesy of Colin M. Caplan.*

Below: Up on the hill behind Donald Grant Mitchell's main house on his Edgewood estate, the views were spectacular. This 1869 photo is looking east over Mitchell's fields that stretched all the way to Edgewood Park and the West River. The fence lines that run left to right mark where roads were eventually opened after Mitchell's death in 1908. This land became the scene of booming residential developments in the years to follow. *Photographed by Rockwood. Courtesy of Colin M. Caplan.*

Mr. Mitchell at eighty is strong and sturdy. He has the delightfully keen eyes that charm, and his broad shoulders bespeak many years to come. He loves his fireplace, his friends, his pictures, his books. He understands the secret of growing old gracefully. Despite a trifling deafness, he is a most charming conversationalist, and the man who shakes his hand will not forget it.

The other large estate in town was called Marvelwood, home to John M. Greist, Westville industrialist and civic leader. Marvelwood eventually spanned seven hundred acres from the sprawling mansion on Forest Road west all the way to the Woodbridge town line. Greist carved Marvelwood out of part of Donald Grant Mitchell's Edgewood estate.

THE SUBTLE BEAUTIES OF NATURE

Connecticut Magazine 3, vol. 8, March 15, 1904

Other than for its beautiful surroundings and commanding situation, Marvelwood, the home of J.M. Greist of New Haven, Connecticut, is remarkable in that it embraces within its domain a compact body of woodland nearly six hundred acres in extent, unbroken by a public road or fence and without a single house or cultivated field to mar its native grandeur, and this immense estate of wild land is entirely enclosed within the territorial limits of the largest city in Connecticut. In no portion of the country east of the plains of the Mississippi is to be found the parallel of Marvelwood in this particular. From the main entrance on Forest Street in New Haven to the farthest western boundary near the town line of Woodbridge, it is distant exactly two and a half miles.

It is interesting to note that the land of which Marvelwood is a part has remained wild since the founding of the New Haven Colony. The original proprietors of New Haven, in common with other early settlements, were particular to guard their woodland privileges. Firewood was considered such an indispensable commodity to the comfort of the early inhabitants that they at once took measures to reserve certain sections of the outlying wild land to be owned in common or equitably divided among the proprietors for purposes of supplying fuel to the infant settlement. Every owner of land in the village either had a corresponding ownership in the woods to the west of the settlement or else had a right in common with others to take wood from the common field. This wood lot was early designated as the Westfield Common Field, and it is so referred to in old deeds and records of the New Haven Colony. In ancient maps and surveys it is designated by that name, and many of the older inhabitants of the city still refer to it as the Westfield Common. In process of time, however, the common ownership became vested in individuals, and at the time Mr. Greist began his purchase there were more than a score of individual owners. The Marvelwood estate, while not coextensive with the ancient boundary of the Common Field, embraces nearly all of the land that did not eventually become cut up into farms and cultivated fields.

In location, contour and nature of soil, the greater portion of this immense estate is admirably adapted to primitive forest conditions. Its native beauty and grandeur are the chief elements of its picturesqueness. As simplicity is the chief element of the sublime, therein lies the chief attraction of the wonderful beauty of this extensive estate. Ave in the immediate vicinity of the house, and where necessary to establish drives and paths, nature's forces are permitted to romp unchecked throughout the extent of its six hundred acres. In this respect its owner has the highest instinct of an artist. At best the most skillful designer of landscape effects can only partially rival the exquisite touch given to a scene by the hands of nature itself. To preserve the grandeur of a native landscape is one thing; to love and appreciate it is another, but when the two concur, the highest expression of art is exemplified.

The constant aim of the owner has been to preserve its primitive aspect. One may search in vain its miles of forest wilds for artificial display or meaningless grouping. Every rock, tree, stream and pond remains today as it was placed by the Great Architect of the Universe. No human distorting of nature's forces has been countenanced in the laying out of the estate. Only in remote instances when nature presented formidable barriers to access to a certain portion of the estate have ancient roads and paths been altered in their course.

The tendency of modern architectural effect, both in landscape gardening and in the rearing of homes, is to magnify at the expense of nature. Most home builders strike a false note when they elaborate upon formality in landscape effect. Nature is the best and surest judge. The owner of Marvelwood has dared to follow in the footsteps of nature, and to stubbornly refrain from employing artificial methods to attain to the beautiful. The result is that one is impressed by its simplicity and pauses in admiration before the silent monuments of nature's own handiwork.

Nowhere throughout its miles of woodland can one find a flower, shrub or plant that is not indigenous to the soil. Beyond the planting of a few rods of hemlock hedge along the north entrance, not a single slip of vegetation has been transplanted. Save where a certain hickory grove near the house needed thinning out to preserve it, not a single stick of living timber has been removed from the soil.

Entering from the street, one approaches the house at a distance of three hundred yards, along an artificial sidewalk that, following the natural ascent of the land, winds among countless oaks, hickories and hemlocks. Following the walk, and at times leaving it to gain a less precipitous ascent, is the crushed stone driveway, with cobble gutters and grass-covered sides.

The hickory grove, through which the walk and drive enters, is a landmark in the western end of the city. It remained in the Dickerman family continuously for more than two hundred years and only passed out of the possession of the family when acquired by Mr. Greist. The date when the ancient grove became established in the soil is not known. To use the language of the law, "The memory of man runneth not the contrary." That the early colonial proprietors suffered the trees to encroach upon cultivated land is attested by the presence of corn rows, which are still traceable in regular lines at intervals through the grove.

Emerging from the precincts of the grove, the walk enters the expansive lawn in its approach to the house. The house stands in a vista of ancient trees, mostly chestnuts, many of which are more than four feet in diameter, through whose friendly avenues of trunks and limbs a merry company of squirrels labor, rollick and scold, fed and protected by the kind-hearted proprietor.

In front of the house and receding from it in every direction, gently sloping toward the street below, is a carpet of lawn of nearly three acres in extent. The lawn in itself presents a field of matchless beauty. Unbroken, save by a single group of hemlocks, it reaches to the eastward a distance of some three hundred feet, and in breadth exceeds four hundred feet.

The group of hemlocks that studs the lawn to the left of the house was set forty years ago by the hand of Mr. Donald G. Mitchell (Ik Marvel), the dean of American letters, whose beautiful estate of Edgewood adjoins Marvelwood on the south. In short, a portion of Marvelwood, particularly that upon which the house stands, was purchased directly of Mr. Mitchell, and for nearly half a century was part of Edgewood.

The situation of the house is beyond question the most striking feature of the Marvelwood estate. From the rich plateau of the western section of the city, the land quickly ascends to the crest of the hill that entirely bounds the view of the western horizon. About two hundred feet above sea level, and upon the highest point of the immediate elevation, stands the costly edifice of Marvelwood. The house faces the east almost as truly as the needle points to the north. The first rays of the sun bathe the house and its surroundings in a glow of golden light and, reaching through the treetops, mellow the western landscape long before the dwellers in the valley below behold its beams.

To the north, and only a short aerial mile removed, is the abrupt precipice of West Rock, the historic eminence that has the proud distinction of having once sheltered two of the judges whose decree of death sent Charles Stuart, King of England, to an ignoble death in Whitehall. Far over against the north, framed in the blue haze of a New England sky, reclines in endless sleep the stony countenance of the "Sleeping Giant," the guardian spirit of Mount Carmel, whose towering summit, reaching far out to sea, gladdens the heart of the homeward-bound sailor.

To the south the eye follows the long expansive bosom of the Sound, flecked with the masts and sails of commerce, and far beyond the white domes and cliffs of Long Island. At the entrance to the harbor, towering heavenward, its whiteness glistening in the summer sun, lifts the historic old lighthouse, whose friendly light of welcome, long since burned out, once guided to a safe harbor the mariners of old, laden with the riches of the Indies.

To the east, spread before the eye like a huge panorama, lies the City of Elms, and miles beyond the range of vision. "Girt by green and silent mountains." To the rear of the house the land sharply descends, and we enter the vale of beeches, whose frosty trunks are scarred and seamed with dates and initials of bygone knights and ladies. Ascending again we follow ancient roads and trails and unexpectedly emerge upon a rocky eminence, four hundred feet above the distant city, and our eye again beholds the panorama mellowed by the increasing distance.

Crossing and recrossing the estate and intersecting each other upon every hand are innumerable old wood roads and trails, many of which have long since become overgrown with grass and brush. Even though the neighboring forest is fast encroaching upon the old roads, they still hold their course through the estate, and turning into them the stroller gains a view down an avenue of noble tree trunks and in the distance is outlined the cedar-capped mountains.

Mr. Greist is devoting much time and expense to the clearing of the old road ways to permit of carriage driving through the estate. Already more than nine miles of the old wood roads have been cleared out and widened to permit of easy passage. When the present scheme of road ways is completed there will be fifteen miles of drives almost entirely improved upon the ancient foundations. Many of these wood roads took their origin in Indian trails, as evidenced by deeds and records. In colonial times the main thoroughfare to the Naugatuck valley crossed the western end of the estate, now an abandoned grass-covered track through the woods. Tradition says it followed a well-established Indian

Taken around 1875 from behind Donald Grant Mitchell's Edgewood homestead, which replaced the old colonial-era house that he originally purchased, West Rock's bare cliffs rise behind Westville village. The Stick-style house was designed by both Mitchell and New Haven architect David R. Brown and appealed more to Mitchell's rustic sense. *Courtesy of the New Haven Museum & Historical Society.*

trail, the same trail over which the representatives of the powerful Mohawk tribe annually made their journey into the county of the Pequot to levy tribute upon that unfortunate and less powerful nation.

In the very heart of the estate, now thickly studded with noble forest trees, many of them at least a century old, is the evidence that some courageous Puritan made an unsuccessful attempt to reduce a portion of the soil to cultivation. In and out among the trees, as in the case of the hickory grove near the house, can be seen traces of a cornfield and dead furrows left by the plow. Standing in the rows and furrows are immense oaks, chestnuts and maples, many of them two feet and more in diameter.

About a year ago, workmen upon the roads had occasion to remove a portion of a dismantled stone wall, the laborious work of an early proprietor. Incorporated in the material of the wall was found a moss-covered stone, upon which the following inscription was rudely but plainly cut,

Librty. 1776. N.H.

The natural beauty of Marvelwood is greatly enhanced by several brooks that find their source in innumerable springs bursting from the wooded hillsides. Roaring Brook, rightly named, is a tumultuous stream rushing through ravines, foaming and bounding over boulders to at length unite its crystal waters with a series of lakes. Mile Brook, though less boisterous, is none the less picturesque. It picks its way through long stretches of primitive forest, bathing the roots of ancient trees with the purity of its waters, and flowing onward serves as a never-failing supply of pure water to an ice pond.

The owner of Marvelwood has never made an effort to stock the estate with game. The plan is to foster and protect the native game rather than to import from other sources. All the native game birds and animals abound, and as no hunting is permitted upon the estate, the increase is noticeable. During the past year several deer have been seen and in the seclusion of the estate it is believed that they will soon become numerous.

Marvelwood is thus an estate of peaceful wilds. The brooks course onward unpolluted; the songbirds nest in peace in the treetops; the noble game birds and animals tread the carpet of the forest unmolested by man; the stately trees proudly rear their heads unscarred by the axe. It is a noble monument to the good taste of him who worships at the shrine of nature, and who lives in peace and friendship with the trees, the birds, the beast of the wild, and joys in the love of nature's handiwork.

GROWTH OF A SUBURB

Westville's growth as a suburb began following the establishment of the first line of public transportation between the village and New Haven. The Fair Haven & Westville Horse Railroad was established between these two localities in 1861, which started the impetus to develop residential lots in Westville. Even after the railway was electrified in 1893–94, most of the houses in town were built clustered around the mills and Main Street, as Whalley Avenue was then known.

This circa 1910 postcard view is looking north down Alden Avenue from near Woodbridge Avenue. Many of the houses on this street were built in the 1890s in response to the opening of the Edgewood Avenue electrified trolley line that ran through here. The developments here were just the beginning of the major residential growth that occurred between 1910 and 1930. *Photographed by the Beck Manufacturing Co. Courtesy of Colin M. Caplan.*

Opening of New Street

New Haven Evening Register, October 18, 1905
Hearing Before Director Coe on Pardee Place Petition

There was a hearing today in city hall before Director of Public Works James B. Coe upon the petition for the opening and grading of Pardee Place, a new street that is proposed to open through the Stephen Pardee estate in Westville. The new street of place is to run north from Fountain Street between Dayton and West Prospect Streets.

The property of the Westville Hotel adjoins the north end of the street and prevents the extension of Pardee Street to Whalley Avenue, which plan has been advocated by some of the people who are interested in the new thoroughfare. The property through which the new street is proposed is in the possession of Anna M. Pardee, but will eventually revert to Grace Hospital, which is also interested in the opening of the street. There was no opposition made to the opening of Pardee Place.

After the death of Donald Grant Mitchell in 1908, a large part of his former estate became available and divided into residential building lots by local development companies. They were keen on developing a suburb with spacious yards, large houses and wide streets.

Westville, New Haven's Beautiful Suburb, Enjoys Remarkable Boom

New Haven Register, June 22, 1913

> Bright homes near placid West River
> Where the patter of little feet
> Spell the sunshine of our schoolhouse
> And the pride and joy of our street

What was years ago a vast stretch of farmlands where early New Haven settlers followed their agricultural pursuits is today undergoing great changes in the making into a residential community, one growing into the other and blending into a harmonious whole. This section where the New Haveners may now see civic pride displayed in home building and what is destined to be an ideal residential spot is in Westville. It lies just across the West River and covers a pretty big tract of ground that which the exception of one or two breaks extends from Chapel Street to Fountain Street. It marks the continuation of the development of the Westville residential section begun several years ago when McKinley Avenue was laid out and fine homes built there. This avenue, because of the fine class of houses built there, has come to be known as the "Hillhouse Avenue of Westville." In the further development of the property in this section, the owners of the land are handling every effort to perpetuate the beauty of this residential spot, preserving the natural beauty and adding to it a class of residences of such architectural beauty as to make it possible to forecast it as resembling, if indeed it does not rival, famous residential sections outside of London. Few localities in or about New Haven compare in natural beauty of setting and refinement of environment with this area of ground that is now being opened up in Westville.

If you have ever crossed the West River into the territory of our closely related neighbors of Westville, you probably know all about the beauty of the location we have tried to describe. Take it from West Chapel Street, after you cross the Chapel Street bridge, and go northward, you have doubtless admired the wide stretch of land lying at the foot of the hills of Marvelwood, and of that beauty spot that most people know well for years, the domicile of "Ik Marvel."

The planners projecting this enterprise of carrying out plans for making this a fine residential section believe that now the time is ripe and their judgment has been found to be correct in the ready response that has come from home builders who have bought building lots and have already built homes on this beautiful tract.

In the early seventies, New Haven people sized up this tract of land for purposes just as have the interests that are now developing it, but for some reason the territory this side of Westville claimed more attention and maybe it was that it was considered "too far out." Now trolleys, handsome concrete bridges over the West River adorned with its electroliers and the street pavement improvements have led the home builders to turn in the direction of Westville.

Edgewood Avenue is one gateway to this ideal home community. Chapel Street furnishes another way of approach. The Edgewood Park leads to the two gateways. The West River skirts sixty feet below this tract of land and the Edgewood parkway with its lake and sunken gardens form an eastern boundary. Someday the park commission will be able to carry out its long talk of development of that park in the building of a park westward the overhanging hills of Marvelwood stretch along. A visitor who made a tour of inspection through this new section of land development declared that it was a "bit of Old Chelsea."

In this section there are three interests selling the building lots and in each case it is controlled by New Haven men, in whom the confidence of the buyer may refer to that extent that they are assured that only such sales are made as will give a guarantee to a purchaser that the house and owners will be of that standing as to give permanency of the character of the place. Already about a dozen houses have been erected and others are in course of construction. Some of the houses are Colonial, but all are in keeping with the environment of the place. There are restrictions as to the building, among these being there are to be no stores or anything usually objectionable to a strictly residential community.

McKinley Avenue, opened five years ago by Messrs. P.R. and H.M. Greist, still offers some very desirable sites for choice homes. The style of houses built upon the lots on this avenue range in price from $6,000 to $12,000. The lots are seventy-five feet front. The avenue runs from Fountain Street to Edgewood Avenue. The homes on this street are very pretty and are fine examples of what will be erected elsewhere on the large area nearby. Among those who now reside on McKinley Avenue are P.R. Greist, Hubert M. Greist, Harrison Hewitt, Charles Lincoln, Ralph Armstrong, Walter Greist, Miss Mary Whiting, E.E. Okeson, Edward Dowson, Clarence Beardsley, Harry A. Leonard, Philip Sellers, E.H. Eggleston and Robert MacArthur Jr.

There has been sold recently lots on McKinley Avenue to Ferdinand Von Beren, the architect, Dr. Burton F. Bishop and Mrs. George Hunter, now of Blake Street. They are to build homes there.

Edgewood Development

The Edgewood Development Company, of which P. Raymond Greist is president, Hubert M. Greist secretary and Albert D. deBussy treasurer, has opened up three thousand front feet of land between Central and Alden Avenues, which is very attractive. This was known as the Osborn-Day property. This parcel of land was opened in the '70s.

After the Civil War there were plans made for opening up this piece of land for residential purposes by the parties then owning the ground. They went so far as to open two streets and plant elm trees. The fruit of the labors of those interested in the land at that time is to be seen today, in the two avenues where the Edgewood Development Company is now offering building sites the elm trees are tall and stately, their wide-spreading branches forming an arch across the streets. It's something not usually found in most localities where land is being opened for building purposes. The beautiful shade trees on both sides of Westwood and Elmwood Roads, which are the names given the streets in the Edgewood Development Company's plot, are one of the attractive features. In addition to the elms, there have been set out catalpas and intersecting catalpas and the elms there have been planted Japanese barberry.

Both Westwood and Elmwood Roads have been curbed and though the building line established by the city is twenty-five feet, the Edgewood Development Company has set the line back five feet more. The Edgewood Development Company's property is centrally situated between Edgewood Avenue and Chapel Street. Electric cars are conveniently near. The style of the houses now being erected on lots sold by the company indicate the high-class residential section the Edgewood Development Company's property is to be. Among those who have built homes on the plot are Charles A. Altman, J.C. Lippincott and Edward E. Peck in Elmwood Road, and in Westwood Road J.K. Dyer, F.C. Kusterer, Harry W. Crawford, Alfred W. Chase and Albert D. deBussy have or are building homes. The Edgewood Development Company restricts houses built on the lots sold by it to a minimum cost of $5,000. There are to be no fences separating the land of the owners and the whole plot will remain open. No stores will be permitted within the areas owned by this company.

Every home being built on this spot is in keeping with the beauty spot.

Frank C. Eberth's Home Sites

Out Edgewood Avenue just a stone's throw from the new Westville public school, Frank C. Eberth and Frank W. Rowley are offering some very choice building lots. The real estate that is being sold by Mr. Eberth is part of the Pope estate, well known to many New Haven people. It is on the south side of Edgewood Avenue and is bounded by Yale and Central Avenues and Chapel Street. There are about fifty lots in this piece of land, which has been cut up for home sites, and representing altogether about two thousand front feet. Some very fine lots are to be obtained on the Yale Avenue side, for this section of the Eberth tract fronts the Edgewood parkway and the scenery is something that would be greatly enjoyed by those looking for a good spot to build a home. The lots on the Yale Avenue side are high and are well adapted for terracing, should the purchaser desire to so arrange his grounds when building. The whole parcel of ground that Mr. Eberth is offering to home builders is high and no filling will be required by anyone buying any of the lots. In selling these lots, Mr. Eberth has placed restrictions such as the class of homes to be built, no dwelling that will cost less than $4,500 being permitted to be erected on any of the lots. There will be no board fences or chicken coops. Walks of cement have been laid and curbs set on Edgewood Avenue, West Rock Road and Central Avenue. Norway maple trees are being set out for shade purposes. All the lots are full fifty feet size. The Edgewood Avenue trolleys pass the grounds. The lots on the Yale Avenue side are thickly wooded and the trees are to be left to be thinned out at the discretion of the purchase of the lots on this side of the property. From the Eberth lots an excellent view of the city and the surrounding country is possible. Several lots have been sold. Mrs. Isabelle W. Seeley has purchased a lot of Mr. Eberth on the northwest corner of Edgewood Avenue and West Rock Road and is building an eight-room stucco residence.

Mr. Eberth has now under construction an eight-room dwelling with all improvements. This is on Edgewood Avenue close by the schoolhouse and will be sold when completed.

Mr. Eberth or a representative may be found on the grounds daily or at his office, 839 Chapel Street.

Part of this big tract of land that has opened up and upon which homes are now being built is known as Rockview and the lots are being sold by the Greist-Leonard Realty Company, of which P. Raymond Greist is president and Harry A. Leonard is secretary, treasurer and general manager. Their well-known interest in the development of Westville is a sufficient guarantee that this tract will be opened up and developed in a first-class manner. There are sixty lots in this property each being almost 50 x 150 feet. The streets have been laid out, curbs and sidewalks laid and trees have been planted on all the property in the fall. A building line has been established, suitable restrictions as to price and character of the houses to be built and the fact that no barns and chicken coops will be allowed on this property makes it an ideal place to buy and build a home. The surroundings are very pleasing, Yale Avenue facing the beautiful Edgewood Park on the east while on the north is a wonderful view of West Rock and to the west the beautiful Woodbridge hills. The owners of this property are reserving a plot in the center that will be used for tennis courts for the use of the purchasers of these lots. There have been several houses erected on the property, the Greist-Leonard Realty Company having two. Mr. A.L. Gates, Mr. Burton L. Tuttle, Mr. George W. Horton each own one family house on West Rock Avenue. Among the other purchasers of property here are W.J. Jordan of the Jordan Company and Mr. Joseph Rice, both of whom have purchased home sites on Central Avenue. Yale Avenue, which is the eastern boundary of the Greist-Leonards tract, is eighty feet wide, while beyond that is the beautiful Edgewood Park. This

This photo was taken of 75 Westwood Road around 1912, just after it was built by Albert deBussy's development company, Lake View Crest Land Development Company. The house was built during Westville's booming development years. Dr. Robert E. Park, a physician at the Elm City Sanitarium, a private hospital located near the medical center, was the first resident. *Courtesy of the New Haven Museum & Historical Society.*

is a very desirable part of Rockview, for it precludes all possibility of any building on the other side of the avenue and gives to the purchaser of lots on the west side of Yale Avenue a fine view of the surrounding scenery. This park drive will extend from Derby Avenue to Central Avenue connecting with Willard Street.

This property covers about fifteen acres and is bounded by Central Avenue on the west, Yale Avenue on the north and east, West Elm Street on the south and is divided by West Rock Avenue running north and south.

People desiring to inspect this property could take the Edgewood Avenue car to West Elm, Burton or Willard Streets and walk one block to the east. A representative of the Greist-Leonard Realty Company is on the property every day and will be pleased to show all interested parties over the property and give them any further information desired.

> The sun is lingering on West Rock
> And caressing the Marvel Hills
> Fain would I dwell in a spot like this
> As my heart with its beauty thrills

RAPID GROWTH OF WESTVILLE IN A FEW YEARS ALMOST WITHOUT A PARALLEL

New Haven Register, March 21, 1915

A trip through Westville these days by the citizen who hasn't been there in six or seven years seems almost like a journey through dreamland. There is as little in the Westville of yesterday, so to speak, as compared to the present-day Westville that the person who strolls or goes by automobile over the fine streets there can hardly realize that it would be possible for a community to develop such a physical change within such a short period of time.

Westville today is justly entitled to be called one of the prettiest outlying districts of any city in Connecticut. The street plan, the beautiful residences, the fine views on all sides and the picturesque location at the foot of historic West Rock tend to make it a suburb of which the city may well feel proud. That the community is enjoying great popularity at the present time and will continue to enjoy it there is no doubt, and a study of the facts incident to the growth and popularity reveals some interesting statistics.

THE GRAND LIST JUMP

One of the most interesting items in this study has to do with the grand list. When you speak of the grand list of a town or a community there is always a chance to make comparisons, and comparisons of grand lists always prove interesting. When a grand list jumps by leaps and bounds it is a sign of prosperity and growth that no other barometer can estimate. Money talks, and when the grand list, which is no more than an estimated value of the real estate and other property of the community, ascends from less than a million dollars to $4,199,880 in half a dozen years, as has the list taking in the thirteenth ward of our city, it means that this increase has been accompanied by a healthy growth. The grand list of Westville for last year, according to the records in the office of the board of assessors, was $2,694,506, showing that within a year the value of the property has increased half a million dollars.

INDUSTRIAL GROWTH

Although the number of industrial plants in Westville is not a remarkably large one, those that make Westville their home boast of the fact that their business has increased steadily for years and in their particular lines they stand well up with any in the country. The biggest plant is that of the Greist Manufacturing Company, employing in normal times about 836 hands with a payroll ranging from $8,000 to $10,000 a week. Most of the employees of this plant as well as the other industrial concerns in Westville make this community their home. The Geometric Tool Company, a company enjoying a great business boom on account of the war orders received, employs about 300 hands and its payroll amount is $4,000 a week, a good deal of which is spent in Westville. The Pond Lily Company, a thriving concern, famous in its line in this community, has between 75 and 100 men and women working in its attractive space at the end of the trolley line and the envelopes distributed every week contain about $1,500 of the coin of the realm. The Parker Paper Mills, working at the present time day and night, employs about 75 hands, and the Forsythe Dyeing Company employs about 50 men and women. The Belden Machine Company completes the list of the Westville manufacturing concerns, employing about 25 persons, with an average payroll of about $300 a week.

The Real Estate Boom

No feature of a community's boom is as important as that pertaining to its real estate. In Westville, a record has been made during the past six years that will be hard to equal anywhere. Building booms are recounted in many parts of the state and are chronicled from time to time as being phenomenal in their growth. In many cases a building boom means nothing but the springing up of a cheap line of houses. In the Westville boom, this is not at all the case. There is a certain refinement to the houses built there during the past six years that calls for expression of approval from all those who have looked the property over lately. For the greater part of the houses are one-family residences, built in good taste. The all-shingle house, the stucco house, the brick house and the combination of stucco and wood are some of the styles of architecture used that combine to make a most pleasing whole.

No section of the city boasts of a prettier and more artistic combination of private dwellings than does Westville, and the *Register* on this page reproduces cuts of some of the many beautiful houses at random and the pictures represent only a small proportion of the comfortable homes of the multitude of New Haven businessmen who have chosen this district for the site of their houses.

Several new streets have been cut through paralleling Alden Avenue and Edgewood Avenue, opening up a territory the advantages of which have been quickly realized by those desiring to live within the city limits and just far enough away from the center of the town to be called real suburbanites, enjoying all the liberties and advantages that go with that title. The Rock

View section of the community is one of the latest to be developed and many fine homes have already been built there. The property has been developed by the Greist-Leonard Company, a corporation that has done its share of contributing to the growth of Westville. The Mitchell estate has sold a big tract of land to the new Edgewood club and the land around McKinley Avenue has been instrumental in developing the property there.

The country club is one of the most pleasant and best equipped for its size in the state, and it is the scene of many large social affairs throughout the year. It has a live set of officers, a membership of about 130 and plans are underway for a further development in its equipment to meet the demands made upon it by its ever-increasing membership. Four tennis courts have been laid out and the land is being prepared for the building of six more, according to officers of the club, making an excellent equipment for all lovers of this popular game. Tennis during the past ten years has enjoyed a wonderful boom and this increase in interest is clearly shown in New Haven. The club is equipped with two bowling alleys and the men and women members of the organization enjoy the alley sport.

President Harrison Hewitt; Vice-president Ralph M. Armstrong; secretary Carleton H. Stevens; treasurer A.D. deBussy. These officers, and H.M. Greist, Frank L. Quimby, George W. Crane, Walter T. Hart and C.H. Morrison, compose the governing board.

In going back to the great increase in land values during the past half dozen years, it is recalled that about in 1909 the property in the so-called Edgewood and Alden Avenue districts, which now includes Rock View and the McKinley Avenue district, all the way up to Forest Street, could be bought for from $7.50 a foot to $10 a foot. If someone had had the foresight to see what was coming, a snug fortune could have been made in half a dozen years just in investing in land there. Today the property sells as high as $50 a foot in some locations and the value is increasing steadily.

THE SCHOOLS

Owing to the growth of Westville, it has of course been necessary to increase the school facilities there until now the district boasts of three first-class schools under the jurisdiction of the school board of Westville. The old Whalley Avenue school is now known as the Mary Frances Benton School, and it is located on the hill just above the post office. This is a ten-room school and it is taxed to its utmost. The Edgewood school on Edgewood Avenue, one of the newest schools in the city limits, is a fine example of the up-to-date public school, and contains eight rooms. The newest school is the L. Wheeler Beecher school, four rooms of which have been opened so far. A

This photograph shows 275 West Elm Street taken shortly after the house was built in 1918. The house was built for Leslie E. Forsyth, who was the treasurer of his family business, the Forsyth Dyeing Company, located at the corner of Whalley Avenue and Fitch Street in Westville. Its curvy design was the work of the New Haven architectural firm of Shiner & Appel. *Courtesy of the New Haven Museum & Historical Society.*

picture of the Beecher school is shown in connection with this story. The other rooms in this building will be thrown open soon.

The Fire Department

The Westville fire department also figures in the growth of Westville, the department being equipped with an automobile fire engine and considerable speed and efficiency. That there have been no serious fires in Westville for some time is attributed to the fact that the firefighting apparatus and its men have been on their jobs at all times.

The Edgewood Civic Association has been an important factor in the development of Westville. This association was formed about six years ago and has taken an active interest in all that stands for civic improvement. The laying of the sidewalks, the cutting through of streets and the general bettering of conditions in the thirteenth ward are the results of this association's activities.

There are four churches in Westville: the St. James Episcopal, the St. Joseph's Roman Catholic, the Congregational and the Methodist Episcopal churches. The Mitchell Memorial Library is one of the district's important institutions.

www.ingramcontent.com/pod-product-compliance
Lightning Source LLC
Chambersburg PA
CBHW060812100426
42813CB00004B/1048